A Taste of Milwaukee

A Taste of Milwaukee

The Muses
Friends of the Museum, Inc.
Milwaukee Public Museum

Book design, Greg Raab
Photography, Jack Jackson, Jack Jackson Studio Ltd.
Specimen selection, Phyllis Reimer, Claudia Jacobson and Donna Holscher
Typesetting, Steve Rademan
Production coordination, Mary Garity
Technical consultation, Tim Schimberg

First printing 10,000 copies   October, 1983
Printed in the United States of America

The Cookbook Committee

All specimens photographed for this book are from the collections of The Milwaukee Public Museum. Proceeds from the sale of *A Taste of Milwaukee* will be used for museum enrichment. Additional copies may be ordered from:

The Muses — Cookbook
Milwaukee Public Museum
800 W. Wells St.
Milwaukee, WI 53233

For your convenience, order blanks are included at the back of the book.

Acknowledgments

The Muses wish to express appreciation to all members of the Milwaukee Public Museum staff who graciously and generously helped with the production of this publication. Special thanks to Kenneth Starr, Director; Claudia Jacobson, Anthropology; James Burnham and Ron Harvey, Conservation; Steve Rademan, Exhibition and Graphics; John Luedtke, John Lundstrom and Howard Madaus, History; Mel Scherbarth, Photography, and especially to Greg Raab and Mary Garity, Publications.

Cover: Woodland Indian containers

The Milwaukee Public Museum has been a center for the research of Woodland Indian cultures and their use of native foods. Many of these foods, such as wild rice, were adopted by later settlers, and when combined with their own specialties have created a distinctive regional cuisine.

Carved wood utensils bearing the beautiful patina of much use, soft woven yarn bags and baskets made of folded birchbark or woven ash strips are distinctive objects made by many Woodland tribes.

In the front, a ceremonial bowl and spoon (Fox) and split ash basket (Oneida). In the back, a birchbark basket (Mascouten), yarn bag (Ojibwa), and wooden spoon (Ottawa).

Contents

A Note to the Cook

We hope you will enjoy the recipes in our book, which have been tested by committee members. *A Taste of Milwaukee* is intended for cooks with basic cooking experience. Unless otherwise specified, the oven should be preheated before baking; eggs used in the recipes are grade A large and all measurements are to be level rather than heaping.

Preface

Pride in tradition, close family relationships, and a strong emphasis on excellence in educational, health, cultural and recreational facilities have provided Milwaukeans with a quality of life considered to be second to none. These same qualities explain some of the reasons why the Milwaukee Public Museum has developed the way it has since 1883, and why it has earned an international reputation for its unique environmental exhibits and scientific programs. The museum serves as a major educational and cultural resource of Milwaukee County.

Friends of the Museum and the MUSES support the museum by providing financial and volunteer assistance, and by promoting museum activities through a large enthusiastic membership.

This publication reflects another aspect of the Milwaukee tradition, that of excellent food served with style and originality, usually at home to suit the season, the host or hostess, and the shared interests of family and friends. We call it gemütlichkeit.

Food is served at brunch, luncheon, dinner, before or after the theatre, après ski, by candle light, exquisitely or informally, aboard a boat, in a sun-filled park, or at tailgate parties at Brewer or Packer games. We offer a taste of Milwaukee.

Jean S. Lindemann

Executive Director
Friends of the Museum, Inc.

Hors d'Oeuvres and Appetizers

European glass

From left to right, water tumbler with gilt scroll work decoration, Italy 1890-
1910. Wine glass with bright gold enamel decoration, Austria-Hungary,
1830-50; shot glass with frosted design of children, Lalique, France 1930;
crystal goblet with fine wheel cut mythological design, Lobemeyer, Vienna,
Austria, 1880. The cheese and fruit are on a plate with cut thumb-print and
sunburst design, Ireland, 1850. The water tumbler of glass has shading from
violet to clear, engraved with floral pattern and monogram, probably
Lobemeyer, Austria, c. 1920. The covered compote with trifoil edge and
honeycomb pattern is from Ireland, made in 1850. In the forefront, a paper-
weight cologne bottle with closely packed canes on a cobalt blue background,
Perthshire, Creiff, Scotland, 1980. The goblet with cut honeycomb design on
the lower areas and transparent enamel decorations on bowl with gold rim
and foot is from Bohemia, 1840. The small vase of clear glass overlaid with
blue glass is cut with a pineapple and fan design, from Czechoslovakia, 1950.
The decanter of clear cut glass is from Holland, 1900.

Hors d'oeuvres & Appetizers

Pam's Chicken Wings

2 dozen chicken wings, tips removed, cut at joints
1 5-oz. bottle soy sauce
1 tsp. prepared mustard
4 Tbs. brown sugar
½ tsp. garlic powder

Mix together the soy sauce, mustard, brown sugar and garlic powder. Put in a shallow baking dish. Add wings, turning to coat all sides. Marinate 2 to 24 hours in refrigerator, turning several times. Bake at 375° for 1 hour, basting while cooking. Serve warm. Yields 24 wings.

Peg Nelson

Boursin Cheese

1 clove garlic, finely minced
2 sprigs parsley, finely minced
1 8-oz. pkg. cream cheese, softened
1 stick butter, softened
¼ tsp. each oregano, thyme, basil

Mix together all ingredients until creamy and smooth. Form into a ball. Refrigerate. Serve with crackers. Yields 1 ball.

Bobbe Blumberg

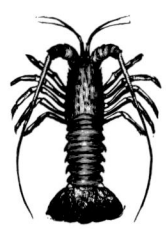

Spinach Balls

2 10-oz. packages frozen, chopped spinach
3 cups packaged bread stuffing for pork, moistened with small amount of water
1 large onion finely chopped
6 eggs, well beaten
¾ cup melted butter
½ cup parmesan cheese
½ to 1 Tbs. pepper
1½ tsp. garlic salt
½ tsp. thyme

Cook spinach. Drain and squeeze dry. Combine with remaining ingredients. Mix well. Chill. Shape into ¾-inch balls. Bake at 325° for 15 to 20 minutes. May be frozen on a cookie sheet, then stored in a plastic bag to have on hand. Thaw slightly. Bake at 325° for 20 to 25 minutes. Serves 20.

Sue Wettengel

Hot Crabmeat Snacks

1 6-oz. can crabmeat
2 Tbs. mayonnaise
1 jar Old English cheese
1 stick butter or margarine
¼ tsp. garlic salt
¼ tsp. seasoned salt
6 English muffins, split

Mix together all ingredients except muffins. Spread on lightly-toasted muffin halves. Cut into fourths. Bake at 375° for 10 to 12 minutes. Yields 4 dozen.

Anonymous

Hors d'oeuvres & Appetizers

Spinach Cheese Appetizers

½ 10-oz. pkg. frozen, chopped
   spinach, thawed and well drained
3 eggs, slightly beaten
1 cup milk
1 cup flour
1 tsp. salt
1 tsp. baking powder
dash of cayenne pepper
1 lb. Monterey Jack or aged
   cheddar cheese, grated
½ stick butter

Mix together the eggs, milk, flour, salt, baking powder and pepper. Add spinach and cheese. Melt butter in a 9x13-inch baking pan. Pour mixture on top. Bake at 350° for 35 minutes. Let cool 30 minutes before cutting into bite-sized pieces. Can be prepared ahead and frozen. Reheat at 350° for 15 minutes. Serve very warm. Yields 15 to 20 appetizers.

Sharon Roderick

Corned Beef Buns

1 12-oz. can corned beef
1 pkg. dry onion soup mix
sour cream
24 small cocktail buns

Mix together the corned beef and onion soup with enough sour cream to hold it together. Fill buns. Bake at 350° for 15 to 20 minutes.

Bobbe Blumberg

Cheese-Shrimp Spread

Can be frozen to keep on hand for company. May be served hot or cold—flavor is excellent either way.

2 8-oz. pkgs. cream cheese,
   softened
1 egg
½ tsp. salt
1 tsp. baking powder
1 tsp. finely-chopped onion
1 Tbs. chili sauce
1 tsp. lemon juice
½ tsp. horseradish
1 4½-oz. can small shrimp,
   drained and mashed
1 6-oz. can water chestnuts,
   drained and chopped

Combine the cream cheese, egg, salt and baking powder. Mix well. Add onion, chili sauce, juice and horseradish. Blend well. Add mashed shrimp and water chestnuts. Mix well. For best flavor, prepare 12 to 24 hours ahead. Then freeze. Thaw before serving and spread cold on crackers. Or spread on crackers. Bake at 375° for 10 minutes. Yields about 3 cups.

Judy De Vries

Hors d'oeuvres & Appetizers

Seafood in Mayonnaise

This can serve four as a first course by spooning onto lettuce-lined plates.

1 6-oz. jar marinated artichokes
2 cups crabmeat or shrimp (fresh, frozen or canned)
½ to 1 cup mayonnaise
1 to 2 tsp. tarragon vinegar
½ tsp. tarragon
¼ cup finely-chopped parsley
¼ cup minced chives

Drain and reserve oil from artichokes. Cut artichokes into small pieces. Mix lightly with shrimp or crabmeat. Blend 3 to 4 teaspoons of the reserved oil with the remaining ingredients. Toss with the seafood mixture. Chill. Serve with wheat crackers with sesame seed. Serves 8 to 10.

Pearl Hunkel

Shrimp Dip

1 4-oz. can small or broken shrimp, mashed
1 cup mild cheddar cheese, grated
¾ cup salad dressing
1 Tbs. minced onion
dash of Worcestershire sauce

Mix together all ingredients. Chill. Serve with rye chips. Yields 1½ cups.

Anonymous

Cheese Straws

Handy to have on hand as they warm up beautifully. Double the recipe as they disappear quickly.

1 stick butter, softened
4 oz. cream cheese, softened
1 cup sifted flour
pinch of salt
1 egg yolk
2 tsp. milk
⅓ cup parmesan cheese
1½ tsp. caraway seeds
1½ tsp. sesame seeds

Blend butter and cream cheese together. Add flour and salt gradually, mixing well. Form into 2 flat rectangles. Wrap in wax paper. Chill overnight. Roll out one rectangle about ¼ inch thick and 3 inches wide, into a long, skinny piece. Mix egg yolk with milk. Brush half on dough. Sprinkle with half the parmesan cheese and caraway seeds. Cut the pastry into strips about ½ to ¾ inches wide by 3 inches long. Repeat the rolling out with second piece of dough, brushing with egg-milk mixture. Sprinkle with remaining cheese and sesame seeds. Place on greased cookie sheets. Bake at 450° for 7 to 9 minutes on upper but not top shelf. Cool. Store in airtight container in refrigerator if served within a week. To freeze, place on a flat tray. When firm, carefully pack in a container and store in freezer. To serve, heat at 350° for about 5 minutes. Yields 28 to 30.

Gloria Stanford

Hors d'oeuvres & Appetizers

Sonora Dip

An unequivocal success for casual entertaining.

1 8-oz. pkg. cream cheese, softened
1 10-oz. can bean dip
10-20 drops hot pepper sauce
1 cup sour cream
½ pkg. dry taco seasoning
½ cup chopped green onions, including green tops
1 cup shredded Monterey Jack cheese

Combine all ingredients except the shredded cheese. Spoon into a 1½-qt. greased casserole dish. Sprinkle on cheese. Bake at 350° for 20 to 25 minutes, until cheese bubbles. Remove from oven. Let stand 5 minutes. Serve with tortilla chips. Serves 15 to 20.

Sandi Moomey

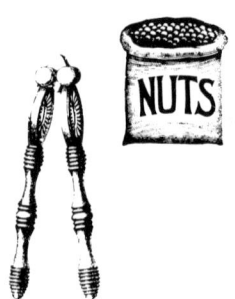

Hot Spinach Appetizers

Make and freeze these ahead of time to have on hand for unexpected company.

2 10-oz. pkgs. frozen, chopped spinach, cooked and drained
2 cups seasoned croutons
1 cup grated parmesan cheese
6 eggs, beaten
¾ cup margarine, softened
salt and pepper to taste

Mix together all ingredients. Put waxed paper on a cookie sheet. Drop mixture by spoonfuls onto paper. Freeze. Remove and store in plastic bags. Freeze. When ready to serve, bake at 350° for 10 to 15 minutes. Yields 5 dozen.

Carol Tishler

Rye Bread Appetizer

1 round (2 lbs.) loaf rye bread
1 small jar Old English cheese
1 tube onion cheese
1 tube bacon cheese
1 tube wine cheese
10 to 12 oz. beer

Cut off top of loaf. Pull out bread, leaving a 1-inch thick shell. In top of a double boiler, melt together the cheeses. Add the beer. Mix well. Pour cheese mixture into bread shell. Bake at 350° for 30 minutes. Use bread chunks for dipping. Serves 6 to 8.

Anonymous

Hors d'oeuvres & Appetizers

Taco Dip

1   10-oz. can enchilada bean dip
3   avocados
2   to 3 jalapeno peppers
1   Tbs. chopped onion
½   tsp. garlic salt
1   cup sour cream
½   cup mayonnaise
½   pkg. taco seasoning
6   to 10 green onions, chopped
8   oz. mozarella or cheddar cheese,
    shredded
2   medium tomatoes, chopped
1   2-oz. can black olives, chopped

On a 12-inch round platter, spread the bean dip very thin. Mash up soft avocados with the jalapeno peppers, onion and garlic salt. Spread over bean dip. Combine the sour cream, mayonnaise and taco seasoning. Spread over avocado mixture. Add layers of remaining ingredients. Serve with crackers or taco-flavored tortilla chips. Can be made day ahead and refrigerated. Serves 10 to 12.

Mary Schmidt

Savory Spinach Dip

1   10-oz. pkg. frozen chopped
    spinach, thawed and well drained
1   pkg. dry vegetable soup mix
1   small onion, minced
1   6-oz. can water chestnuts,

    drained and diced
1   cup mayonnaise
1   cup sour cream
pinch of nutmeg
1   round sour dough bread loaf

Mix together all ingredients except bread. Refrigerate overnight to blend flavors. Hollow out the loaf of bread. Retain hollowed out part and cut into chunks. When ready to serve, put dip into bread shell. Put bread chunks around and serve. Dip may also be served with raw vegetables, corn chips or crackers. Serves 12 to 15.

Gloria Mitchelson

•

Appetizers are a part of every national cuisine. The Italians have "antipasto" the Scandinavians "smorgasboard" the French the "hors d' oeuvres" and "canape." The difference between the two French appetizers is that the hors d' oeuvres is served alone whereas the canape should have a base or"couch" such as bread, cracker or pastry which can be picked up with the fingers.

•

11

Hors d'oeuvres & Appetizers

Spinach Appetizer

2 10-oz. pkg. frozen, chopped spinach
3 Tbs. butter or margarine
1 small onion, diced
¼ lb. fresh mushrooms, sliced or 1 4-oz. can, drained
4 eggs
½ cup grated parmesan cheese, divided in half
1 10-oz. can undiluted cream of mushroom soup
¼ cup seasoned bread crumbs
⅛ tsp. each of pepper, basil and oregano

Thaw spinach in a colander. Squeeze out liquid. Saute onion and mushrooms in butter until onion is limp but not brown. In a mixing bowl beat eggs. Add ¼ cup cheese, soup, crumbs and seasonings. Mix thoroughly. Add spinach and onion mixture. Mix well. Pour into a 9x13-inch glass baking dish which has been sprayed with a nonstick vegetable oil spray. Sprinkle evenly with remaining cheese. Bake at 325° for 35 minutes or until set. Cool. Cut into small squares. Can be served warm or cool. Can be baked in a 7x11-inch pan for thicker squares and served as a side-dish vegetable. Add 10 minutes to cooking time. Yields 18 to 24 squares.

Ellen Stern

Herbed Cheese Spread

This spread's flavor improves with age.

¾ lb. feta cheese
1 8-oz. pkg. cream cheese, cubed
¼ small onion, grated
1 tsp. anchovy paste
1 tsp. ground caraway seed
½ tsp. dry mustard
2 tsp. sweet Hungarian paprika
5 Tbs. beer
garnish:
1 red pepper, seeded, sliced into rings
1 green pepper, sliced into rings
radishes
thinly sliced pumpernickel bread

Combine first 8 ingredients in a blender or food processor. Put in a tight-fitting covered container. Refrigerate for 24 hours to blend flavors. Serve on a tray with pepper rings, radish rosettes and bread. Yields 1 pint.

Audrienne Eder

Hors d'oeuvres & Appetizers

Savory Bread Sticks

A make-ahead snack to have on hand for emergencies.

Thin bread sticks, enough to fill an 8-inch square baking dish
1 cup oil
2 Tbs. garlic powder
½ Tbs. onion salt
1 Tbs. Worcestershire sauce
1 Tbs. monosodium glutamate

Mix together the oil and seasonings. Pour over bread sticks in baking dish. Mix gently. Bake at 250° for 1½ hours, stirring occasionally. Cool. Store in an airtight container. Yields 4 to 5 cups.

Gloria Mitchelson

Dilly of a Dip

Use as a dip for an assortment of raw vegetables.

⅔ cup sour cream
⅔ cup non-fat yogurt or mayonnaise
1-2 tsp. dill weed
1 tsp. each parsley flakes, onion flakes, beau monde seasoning
3 drops hot pepper sauce
1 tsp. Worcestershire sauce
dash of garlic powder
salt and pepper to taste

Blend together all ingredients. Chill overnight. Yields 1½ cups.

Kathryn Arthur

Spinach-Oyster Dip

3 10-oz. pkgs. frozen chopped spinach
2 9¼-oz. pkgs. frozen oysters or 1½ pts. fresh
1 cup butter
½ cup flour
2 cloves garlic, minced
1½ tsp. salt
½ tsp. pepper
⅓ cup onion flakes
½ cup chopped parsley

Cook spinach. Drain and set aside. Cook oysters in juice about 3 minutes. Drain and chop, reserving 1 cup oyster water, adding water if necessary to make 1 cup. Melt butter. Stir in flour. Cook over low heat for 5 minutes. Blend in reserved oyster water, garlic and salt and pepper. Stir until smooth. Stir in onion flakes, parsley, spinach and oysters. Stir until thickened. Serve in a chafing dish with crackers on the side. Can be made day ahead. Heat in a casserole dish at 350° for 20 minutes. Serves 24. Recipe can be cut in ⅓ to serve 8.

Carol Dickson

Hors d'oeuvres & Appetizers

Cheese Tarts

A mild-flavored appetizer that you can spice up with your own choice of seasonings.

1 cup cottage cheese
1 egg
1 pkg. puff pastry

Beat together cottage cheese and egg. Roll sheets of puff pastry to 1/16-inch thickness. Cut into 2½-inch circles. In center of each circle place ½ teaspoon of cheese mixture. Fold circle in half. Moisten edges and press to seal. Crimp edges as for a pie. Place on greased baking sheets. Bake at 400° for 15 to 20 minutes or until golden. Serve warm. May be prepared and frozen before baking. Yields 30 to 40 appetizers.

Anonymous

Marge's Skiers Snack

¾ to 1 cup oil
1 pkg. buttermilk salad dressing mix
½ tsp. garlic salt
1 large pkg. oyster crackers

Mix together the oil, salad mix and garlic salt in a large bowl. Add crackers and toss to coat well. Store in an airtight container. Yields 4 cups.

Sue Wettengel

Chili Con Queso

A hot dip directly from New Mexico.

1 lb. process cheese, cubed
½ lb. cheddar cheese, grated
1 4-oz. can chili peppers, drained and chopped
¼ to ⅓ cup chopped green onions
¼ tsp. garlic powder
¼ tsp. onion salt
¼ tsp. hot pepper sauce

Combine all ingredients. Heat in a double boiler until cheese melts. If cheese curdles, add a pinch of baking soda. Serve and keep warm in a chafing dish. Serve with tortilla or corn chips. Serves 15 to 20.

Sue Wettengel

Hors d'oeuvres & Appetizers

Artichoke Dip

A fast hors d' oeuvres for artichoke lovers.

1 cup mayonnaise
1 cup grated fresh parmesan cheese
1 10½-oz. can artichoke hearts, quartered, drained

Combine the mayonnaise and cheese. Mix well. Add artichoke. Mix. Bake in a shallow pan at 350° for 20 to 25 minutes. Serve with crackers. Serves 6.

Sue Wettengel

Cheese Ball

2 3-oz. pkgs. cream cheese, softened
2 tsp. light cream
⅔ cup chopped, ripe olives
6 slices bacon, fried, drained and chopped
½ tsp. Worcestershire sauce
¼ cup chopped walnuts

Mix cream cheese with cream. Add remainig ingredients. Shape into a ball and chill. Serve with your favorite crackers.

Mary Zastrow

Coconut Surprises

1 3-oz. pkg. cream cheese, softened
1 tsp. each grated orange and lemon rinds or ½ tsp. curry powder
1 tsp. chopped walnuts
¼ cup toasted, flaked coconut

Beat cheese until light and fluffy. Add next two ingredients. Shape into 20 balls, about ½ teaspoon each. Roll in coconut. Chill. Yields 20 appetizers.

Gloria Schranz

Hors d'oeuvres & Appetizers

Tasty Taco Canape

A spread for a young crowd or an informal gathering as it is eaten with the fingers and may be a bit messy.

2   8-oz. pkg. cream cheese
1   8-oz. carton small-curd cottage cheese
1   cup sour cream
1   pkg. dry taco mix
1   4-oz. pkg. shredded sharp or taco cheese
¼   head iceberg lettuce, shredded
10 black olives, pitted and chopped
½   green pepper, seeded and chopped
1   medium onion, chopped
2   small tomatoes, chopped

Mix together cream cheese, cottage cheese and sour cream. Spread on a large round platter. Sprinkle with taco mix. Pile on remaining ingredients. Serve with tortilla chips or corn chips. Serves 8 to 10.

Gloria Mitchelson

Hot Potato Skins

A popular appetizer or side dish.

2 baked potatoes
2 Tbs. butter, melted
garlic salt
paprika
grated cheese
bacon bits
pimiento
chopped parsley
sour cream

Cut baked potatoes in half lengthwise. Scoop out insides. Place skins on a baking sheet. Brush with butter. Sprinkle on garlic salt and paprika. Bake at 400° for 20 minutes. Sprinkle on remaining ingredients of your choice. Serves 2 to 4.

Ann Hill

Spinach Dip

This keeps 3 to 4 days in refrigerator.

1 10-oz. pkg. frozen, chopped spinach, thawed and drained
¾ cup mayonnaise
¼ cup sour cream
1 cup dry shredded parsley
½ cup chopped onion

Mix together all ingredients until well blended. Chill 12 hours or overnight. Serve with raw vegetables.

Judy De Vries

Hors d'oeuvres & Appetizers

Mushroom Turnovers

Can be made ahead, frozen individually and stored in freezer.

*2 sticks (½ lb.) butter, softened
8 oz. cream cheese, softened
1¾ cups sifted all-purpose flour
pinch of salt*

*filling:
1 large onion, finely chopped
½ lb. mushrooms, finely chopped
3 Tbs. butter
1/8 tsp. thyme
½ tsp. salt
⅛ tsp. black or white pepper
1 Tbs. flour
¼ cup sour cream
1 Tbs. dry sherry or dry vermouth
1 egg beaten, thinned with 1 Tbs. water
paprika (optional)*

To make pastry, blend together the butter and cream cheese. Add flour and salt, mixing thoroughly with a wooden spoon or food processor. Divide into 2 portions. Wrap and chill at least 4 hours.

To make filling, melt butter in a large skillet. Add onion. Saute lightly for 10 minutes. Add mushrooms. Cook another 10 minutes. Add seasonings. Blend in flour. Add sour cream and sherry. Cook until mixture thickens, about 5 to 10 minutes. Cool.

Roll out pastry to about ⅛ -inch thickness, using a rolling pin with sleeve. Flour it and board as needed. Cut the pastry into 2½-inch rounds. Put a teaspoon of filling in center of each circle. Fold pastry over to form a half-moon shape. Press edges together with tines of a fork, dipping tines in flour to prevent sticking. With same fork, prick each pastry. Place on ungreased cookie sheets. Chill 30 minutes. Brush tops with egg-water mixture dusting lightly with paprika. Bake on middle shelf of oven at 425° for 15 to 20 minutes. Serve immediately. These hold up well on a warming tray. If frozen, brush tops with egg-water mixture and dust with paprika after removing from freezer. Bake at 425° for 20 to 25 minutes. Yields 3 dozen.

Gloria Stanford

Hors d'oeuvres & Appetizers

Tyropita (Cheese-Filled Tidbits)

1 pkg. *frozen filo dough, thawed
according to package directions*
¼ *cup fresh parsley, stems
removed*
½ *lb. feta cheese, cut in 1-inch
squares*
1 *egg*
3 *Tbs. unsalted butter, melted*
2 *8-oz. pkgs. cream cheese, cut in
1-inch squares*
1 *cup unsalted butter, melted*

Use steel blade of food processor.
Process parsley until minced. Add
the feta cheese. Process until crumbly. Add egg and 3 tablespoons of
melted butter. Process. Add cream
cheese through feed tube, a few
pieces at a time. Process until
smooth. Brush one sheet of dough
with butter. Top with another sheet.
Brush with butter. Cut into 6 or 7
pieces the short way. Place 1
teaspoon of cheese mixture at one
end and fold into triangles as in
folding a flag. Pinch dough to seal.
Continue until all dough and filling
are used. Place on a lightly greased
cookie sheet. Brush with melted
butter. Bake at 400° for 10 minutes,
or until golden. Can be frozen on
cookie sheets and kept up to 4
weeks. Do not brush with melted
butter until cooking time. Then bake
at 400° for 15 to 20 minutes, or until
thawed and golden.
Yields 120 pieces.

Elizabeth Pleier

Walking Tostada

A hot appetizer that will be enjoyed
by both adults and the younger
crowd.
1 *1-lb. can refried beans*
1 *6-oz. can guacamole or
guacamole dip*
1 *8-oz. carton sour cream*
4 *oz. chopped green chili peppers,
drained*
1 *4-oz. can chopped black olives*
1 *cup diced tomatoes, drained on
toweling*
3 *to 4 green onions, chopped*
1½ *cups shredded cheddar cheese*
tortilla chips

Layer ingredients in order in a
10-inch pie pan or baking dish. Bake
at 250 to 300° until hot, about 10 to
15 minutes. Serve with tortilla chips.
Serves 10 to 12.

Judy Heiligenstein

Notes

Soups

Continental decorative and utilitarian wares

In the back row, a long stemmed wine glass with vintage wheel cut design and gilding from Bohemia, 1885-1900; a green glass goblet with enamel decoration for the Hungarian market, from Bohemia, 1900-1914; a gilt bronze doré garniture bowl on an onyx base, from France, 1890-1900; a green glass roemer decorated with two types of gold over enamel, from Bohemia, 1830-1850; and an engraved green glass wine ewer with pewter mountings, from Germany, 1825-1875.

Decorative items in the middle row include a damascene bronze dinner bell in the shape of a turtle from Seville, Spain, 1960; and a sterling silver ladle, from Prague, Austria — Hungary, 1851.

In the front row is an 8½″ porcelain plate of the Pan Slavic Kremlin service with the Imperial eagle at the center and the text "Nicholas, Czar and Sovereign of All Russians," made in the Imperial Porcelain Factory, St. Petersburg, 1825; a porcelain napkin ring from Erinbringfra, Norway, 1900; and a 9½″ porcelain plate of another Pan Slavic Kremlin service with four Imperial eagles in the border, from the Imperial Porcelain Factory, St. Petersburg, 1825-1855.

Soups

Seafood Chowder

Several slices salt pork, diced
2 Tbs. minced onion
2 Tbs. butter
1/4 lb. fresh mushrooms, sliced
3 cups milk
1 cup heavy cream
1 1/2 tsp. grated lemon peel
1/2 tsp. salt
1/4 tsp. mace
1/8 to 1/4 tsp. pepper
1/8 tsp. basil
1 pt. oysters, fresh, frozen or
    canned
1/2 lb. shrimp, shelled and cleaned
1/4 lb. flaked crabmeat (fresh, frozen
    or canned)
2 tsp. fresh chopped parsley
1 egg yolk
2 tsp. dry sherry

Saute salt pork until brown. Drain on paper towel. Saute onions in some of the fat and butter. Add mushrooms. Cook over low heat until coated with butter. Add milk and all but 2 tablespoons of cream. Add lemon peel and seasonings. Continue to heat slowly until liquid is very hot and begins to bubble. Add oysters, shrimp and crabmeat. Heat thoroughly until edges of oysters begin to curl and shrimp turns pink, about 5 minutes. Add parsley. Beat remaining cream with egg yolk. Add to soup, stirring vigorously to prevent cooking of egg. Heat, stirring constantly, about 2 more minutes. Stir in sherry. Serve immediately sprinkled with salt pork. Serves 6.

Marion Wolfe

Chilled Cream of Cucumber Soup

2 medium cucumbers
1 cup water
2 slices onion
1/4 tsp. salt
1/8 tsp. white pepper
1/4 cup flour
2 cups chicken broth
1 small bay leaf
1/2 to 1 Tbs. dill weed
3/4 cup sour cream

Pare cucumbers. Slice in half lengthwise. Scoop out seeds. Slice into 1/2-inch pieces. Cook cucumbers with the water, onions, salt and pepper until very soft. Mix in an electric blender until smooth. In a 2-quart saucepan mix flour and 1/2 cup chicken broth until smooth. Add remaining chicken broth, cucumber puree and bay leaf. Heat over low heat, stirring constantly. Add dill weed. Simmer 4 minutes. Remove bay leaf. Chill in a covered container. At serving time, gently stir in sour cream. Serve very cold, garnished with cucumber slices or a dash of dill weed. Serves 6 to 8.

Deborah Holbrook

Soups

Mulligatawney Soup

Originally a highly-seasoned Indian soup whose name means "pepper water."

3 chicken breasts, skinned and
   boned
2 qts. water
1 bay leaf
1 Tbs. salt
10 whole peppercorns
1 Tbs. minced onion
2 Tbs. margarine
1 large carrot, sliced
1 large tart apple, diced (add lemon
   juice to a sweeter apple)
1½ tsp. curry powder
¾ tsp. chili powder
½ tsp. coriander
¼ tsp. mace
1½ cups pineapple juice
1 Tbs. sugar
2 Tbs. cornstarch

In a large soup kettle, combine the chicken, water, bay leaf, salt, peppercorns and onion. Simmer, covered, for 1½ hours or until chicken is tender. Strain into a bowl, saving chicken and broth. In same kettle, melt margarine. Add carrot and apple. Saute until soft. Add curry, chili, coriander and mace. Cook 1 minute. Add juice, 4½ cups of reserved broth and sugar. Cover. Simmer for 15 to 20 minutes. Add chicken, cut into bite-sized pieces. Simmer 30 minutes more. add cornstarch which has been mixed with ¼ cup water. Simmer until clear and thickened slightly. Garnish with parsley, if desired. Serves 8 to 10.

Peg Nelson

•

New England clam chowder dates back to colonial times, the original recipe being a combination of clams and a cream sauce. Tomatoes were added at a later time and now is usually called Manhattan Clam Chowder.

•

Soups

Mushroom Chowder

A delicious, buttery-flavored soup for the devout mushroom lover.

1 lb. fresh mushrooms, rinsed, dried and sliced
½ cup butter or margarine
½ cup chopped onion
1 cup diced potatoes
1 cup finely chopped celery
½ cup diced carrots
1¾ tsp. salt
½ tsp. freshly ground black pepper
1 Tbs. flour
2 Tbs. cold water
3 cups boiling water
1 cup light cream or milk
½ cup grated parmesan cheese

In a large saucepan, melt butter. Add the onion. Saute until golden. Add the mushrooms, remaining vegetables, salt and pepper. Cover. Simmer 15 to 20 minutes or until vegetables are tender. Combine the flour and cold water. Slowly stir into vegetable mixture. Add the boiling water. Simmer 10 minutes longer. Just before serving, stir in the cream and cheese. Heat only until hot. Do not boil. Serves 8.

Marie Grayer

Hearty Soup

1 qt. real chicken stock or 2 10-oz. cans chicken broth
½ lb. fresh broccoli or 1 10-oz. pkg. frozen broccoli, thawed
1 cup chopped cabbage
2 carrots, sliced
1 large potato, quartered and sliced
1 large onion, diced
3 Tbs. chicken fat roux (approximate)
½ pt. whipping cream or half and half
dash of garlic powder
salt and pepper to taste

Dice broccoli. Cook broccoli, cabbage, carrots, onion and potato in chicken stock until tender, about 15 minutes. Make a roux by combining chicken fat (or butter or margarine) with an equal amount of flour. Add roux to vegetable mixture. Cook an additional 25 minutes. Add cream, being careful not to boil. Add seasonings. If soup is too thick, additional cream or milk may be added. Serves 4 to 6.

Patricia Dulski

Soups

French Onion Soup au Gratin

Addition of carrots enhances flavor of this classic soup.

¼ cup butter
4 large onions, chopped
¼ cup flour
7 cups beef consomme
1 cup dry white wine
2 large carrots, peeled and sliced
French bread slices, ¾-inch thick, toasted
Swiss cheese, cut into ¼-inch thick slices

Melt butter in a 2½-quart saucepan. Add onions. Cook until soft and transparent. Blend in flour. Add consomme, wine and carrots. Cover. Simmer for 20 minutes. Ladle soup into individual ovenproof mugs. Place a bread slice on top of each, then a slice of cheese. Cheese should extend over sides of mug. Bake at 425° for 20 minutes or until cheese is soft and golden brown.
Serves 6 to 8.

Deborah Holbrook

Cream of Mushroom Soup

3 Tbs. butter
1 small onion, finely chopped
1½ cups finely chopped fresh mushrooms
3 Tbs. flour
2½ cups water
salt and pepper to taste
1 bay leaf
½ to 1 cup cream, or half and half or whipping cream
2 tsp. finely chopped chives

Melt 2 tablespoons of butter in a saucepan. Saute onion and mushrooms over a low fire for 5 minutes. Blend in flour. Add water and seasonings, stirring until mixture comes to a boil. Add bay leaf. Simmer for 10 to 15 minutes. Remove bay leaf. Beat in remaining butter. Add cream and chives. Simmer a few minutes longer. Serve piping hot. Serves 4.

Virginia Feind

Soups

Fruit Soup

Serve this as a first course at a summer luncheon. Also refreshing as a soft, not too sweet desert. Garnish with whole strawberries.

1 qt. fresh strawberries or raspberries
1 cup orange juice
1½ Tbs. cornstarch
½ cup sugar
1 Tbs. lemon juice
1 cup buttermilk

Mix berries, juice and cornstarch in a blender until very smooth. Bring to a quick boil in a saucepan stirring to prevent lumps. Remove from heat and add remaining ingredients. Cover and chill. Keeps several days refrigerated. Serves 6.

Peg Nelson

•

In the colder areas of Colonial America, soup was frozen while still in a kettle. A paddle with a hole in it was stuck into the pot and when solid, the entire mass was removed and hung in a shed. Chunks could be cut off and reheated as needed.

•

Fish Chowder

1½ to 2 lbs. frozen fish
2 small potatoes, chopped
1 10-oz. can potato soup
1 medium onion, minced
3 stalks celery, minced
2 Tbs. butter
1 10-oz. pkg. frozen mixed vegetables
¼ tsp. salt
⅛ tsp. pepper
½ tsp. thyme
tarragon or rosemary to taste
1 can water
1 cup milk or cream

Saute onions and celery until soft. Add all remainig ingredients except milk. Fish may be added frozen, breaking up pieces as it defrosts. Simmer for 30 minutes or until potatoes are done. Add milk or cream just before serving. Bring just to boiling. Serves 6 to 8.

Julie Revane

Soups

A Simple Soup

3 to 4 large carrots, sliced ½ inch
   thick
1 cup chopped celery
1 large potato, chopped
½ large onion, chopped
3 cups water
2 Tbs. margarine
½ tsp. Italian seasoning (basil,
   oregano, crushed fennel)
½ tsp. pepper
⅛ tsp. garlic powder
1 28-oz. can tomatoes
½ bag frozen mixed vegetables
salt to taste

In a 4-quart saucepan, combine carrots, celery, potato, onion, water, margarine and seasonings. Bring to boil. Cover. Simmer for 20 minutes. Add tomatoes and mixed vegetables. Cook uncovered for 10 minutes more. Add rice or barley if you wish. Serves 6 to 8.

Edith Aschauer

Senate Bean Soup

A hearty soup that is served in the United States Senate Cafeteria.
Serve in earthenware pots with garlic bread.

1 lb. of marrow beans (large navy
   beans)
3 qts. cold water
3 medium potatoes, cooked and
   mashed
6 stalks celery, chopped
¼ cup chopped parsley
2 medium onions, minced
2 cloves garlic, minced
2-lbs. ham hock
salt and pepper

Soak beans in water overnight. Drain. Cook beans in fresh water to cover about 1 hour, or until beans are tender. Drain. Add the 3 quarts of water and remaining ingredients. Season to taste, depending on saltiness of ham hock. Cook slowly for 2 hours, stirring occasionally to prevent scorching. Remove meat from bones, cutting into small pieces. Add meat to soup. Yields about 2 quarts.

Julie Revane

Soups

Summer Chowder

3   leeks, white part only, sliced
1   cup cut green beans
1   cup lima beans
1   cup tomatoes, peeled, seeded
     and sliced
½   cup diced eggplant
½   cup diced carrot
½   cup corn
½   cup chopped okra (optional)
¼   cup red pepper, julienne cut
¼   cup chopped green pepper
¼   cup chopped celery
2   10-oz. cans beef bouillon
1⅔ cups milk
2   Tbs. melted butter
2   Tbs. cornstarch
salt, pepper and marjoram to taste

In a large kettle, saute leeks in a little oil until limp. Add vegetables and bouillon. Bring to a boil. Simmer 30 minutes. Add milk. Simmer uncovered for 20 minutes. Add butter and cornstarch mixed with 1 cup of broth from kettle. Add seasonings. Simmer 10 more minutes before serving. Serves 8 to 10.

Elizabeth Pleier

Fundy-Style Clam Chowder

2   Tbs. diced bacon
½   cup chopped onion
1   cup diced potatoes
2   cups water
1   pt. clams plus liquid or 1   20-oz.
     can clams
1   large can evaporated milk
1   tsp. salt
¼   tsp. white pepper

Fry bacon until crisp. Remove from pan and save for garnish. Saute onions in bacon fat until tender but not brown. Combine potatoes and onions in a deep saucepan. Add water. Simmer until potatoes are cooked, about 15 minutes. Stir in remaining ingredients. Heat but do not boil. Garnish with bacon.
Serves 6.

Jo Ann Beightol

•

Soup was one of America's first "convenience foods" as a pot was usually left simmering on the fire all day. If there was no time to cook, there was usually hot soup available, with leftover vegetables and meats added daily.

•

29

Soups

Speedy Gazpacho

An easy, quick version with an excellent flavor. Serve it for a summer luncheon along with muffins and a green salad.

2 10¾-oz. cans condensed tomato soup
2 envelopes instant beef broth
¼ cup red wine vinegar
1 Tbs. vegetable oil
1 tsp. salt
1 tsp. Worcestershire sauce
dash of hot pepper sauce
2 medium tomatoes, chopped
¼ cup chopped green pepper
2 Tbs. minced onion

About 3 hours ahead of serving time, pour undiluted tomato soup into a large bowl. In a small saucepan over high heat, heat 2 soup cans of water to boiling. Remove from heat and add beef broth, stirring until dissolved. Add broth to tomato soup, stirring until well blended. Stir in remaining ingredients. Cover. Refrigerate until serving time. Garnish with peeled and thinly-sliced cucumbers, sliced, pitted black olives or corn chips. Serves 4 to 6.

Peg Nelson

Kohlrabi Soup

1 cup chopped onion
4 Tbs. butter
1 13¾-oz. can chicken broth
4 medium kohlrabi, pared and sliced (about 3 cups)
1½ cups milk
salt and pepper to taste
snipped chives

In a saucepan, cook onion in butter until tender but not brown. Add broth and kohlrabi. Cover. Simmer until kohlrabi is tender, about 20 minutes. Pour into a blender. Cover. Blend until smooth. Return mixture to saucepan. Add milk, salt and pepper. Heat through. Serve garnished with chives. Serves 6.

Jo Anne Shelwat

Soups

Hick's Landing Cream of Zucchini Soup

A tasty way to use a bumper crop of zucchini from your garden.

4 cups cubed zucchini, peeled
½ cup water
½ tsp. salt
½ tsp. sugar
½ small onion, chopped
2 Tbs. butter
2 Tbs. flour
½ tsp. salt
dash of pepper
2 cups milk

Simmer zucchini, water, ½ teaspoon salt and sugar until zucchini is tender. Put zucchini mixture in a blender and puree. Cook onion in butter until transparent. Blend in flour, ½ teaspoon salt, pepper and milk. Add pureed zucchini mixture. Stir until thickened. Garnish with diced pimiento, chopped dill or chopped parsley, if you wish. Serve hot with crackers and cheese wafers, if desired. Serves 4 to 6.

Carol Tishler

Soup for a Cold Winter Day

3 cups tomato juice
3 cups water
3 packets rich brown seasoning mix and broth
1 cup sliced celery
1 cup sliced fresh mushrooms
1 cup shredded red cabbage
2 Tbs. onion flakes or fresh minced onion
1 clove garlic, minced
1 tsp. basil, crushed
salt and freshly ground black pepper to taste
1½ cups sliced zucchini
1 cup French-cut green beans
¼ cup peas, optional

Place first 10 ingredients in a large pot. Cover. Simmer 45 to 60 minutes. Add zucchini, beans and peas the last 10 to 15 minutes of cooking time. Serves 6.

Priscilla Heinecke

Soups

Marrow Dumplings

A good addition to your homemade beef or chicken soup.

4 Tbs. fresh marrow, strained
   through a sieve
2 Tbs. butter
3 eggs, beaten
½ tsp. salt
dash of pepper
¼ tsp. nutmeg
2 Tbs. minced parsley
1 cup fine bread crumbs or Italian
   bread crumbs
½ tsp. baking powder

Combine all ingredients. Beat until smooth, using enough bread crumbs to hold mixture together. Form into small, marble-sized balls. Cook in boiling broth for 10 to 15 minutes. Serves 4 or more.

Rose Marie Barber

Quick Spinach Vichyssoise

Add nutmeg and sherry wine to perk up flavor if you wish.

2 10-oz. cans cream of potato soup
2 soup cans milk
1 10-oz. pkg. frozen, chopped spinach or fresh cooked spinach
2 Tbs. chopped chives
1 tsp. fresh basil, crumbled
⅛ tsp. freshly ground pepper
1 cup sour cream
milk

In medium saucepan, combine soup, milk, spinach, chives, basil and pepper. Heat until spinach is thawed and soup is hot. Bring to boiling over low heat. Reduce heat. Simmer 1 minute. Remove from heat. Pour half of mixture into a blender. Cover. Blend until smooth. Pour into a large bowl. Repeat with other half. Stir in sour cream. Mix until smooth. Cover. Refrigerate until well chilled, about 4 hours. Thin with a small amount of milk if necessary. Serve in soup bowls garnished with a small dollop of sour cream and a sprinkle of chives. Serves 8.

Priscilla Heinecke

Notes

Breads

Washo basketry

The many Indian tribes of the American West use a wide range of natural grains, nuts, seeds and berries in their diet. These are often in the form of unleavened breads. The land also provides the raw materials to make basketry in which to gather, process and store these foods.

Washo basketry is an integral part of the environment of the Great Basin. It not only comes from the land, but is used to gather its produce and in nearly every aspect of the Washo life. Dozens of steps are used to make a basket and then process the food collected with it, and more than one type of basket is used. The Washo are reknowned for the high quality and bold design of their baskets — even in the most utilitarian object.

Breads

English Muffin Loaves

Slice and toast and serve with butter and jam for a special breakfast treat.

3 cups flour
2 pkgs. yeast
1 Tbs. sugar
2 tsp. salt
¼ tsp. baking soda
2 cups milk
½ cup water
1 to 1½ cups raisins, optional
2½ to 3 cups flour
cornmeal

Combine the flour, yeast, sugar, salt and baking soda. Mix well. In a saucepan heat the milk and water to 120 to 130°. Add to the dry ingredients. Beat well. Add the raisins. Stir in enough of the flour to make a stiff batter. Spoon into 2 8½x4½-inch pans that have been greased and sprinkled with cornmeal. Sprinkle tops with additional cornmeal. Cover and let rise in a warm place for 45 minutes. Bake at 400° for 25 minutes. Remove from pans immediately. Let cool. Yields 2 loaves.

Donna Holscher

Yeast Dinner Rolls

½ cup shortening
3 Tbs. sugar
1 tsp. salt
½ cup boiling water
2 eggs, beaten
1 ⅔-oz. yeast cake
½ cup lukewarm water
3 cups sifted flour
½ cup butter, melted

In a bowl combine the shortening, sugar, salt and boiling water. Mix well. Cool. Add eggs. Beat well. Dissolve the yeast in the ½ cup water. Add to the mixture. Add 1½ cups flour. Beat well with a mixer. Add remaining 1½ cups flour, mixing well with a spoon. Place in a greased bowl. Cover and refrigerate for 2 hours. Roll or pat out onto a floured surface to ¼-inch thickness. Cut with a 2-inch round cutter. Brush each piece with melted butter and fold in half. Set close together in an ungreased pan. Cover and let rise for 2 hours. Bake at 400° for 14 minutes. Yields 30 to 36.

Marion Wolfe

Breads

Sour Cream Rolls

1 oz. fresh yeast dissolved in 1 Tbs. warm water
1 cup sour cream or sour half and half
2 egg yolks
1 tsp. vanilla
3½ cups sifted all-purpose flour
1 tsp. salt
½ lb. butter
⅔ to 1 cup sugar

icing:
   4 Tbs. butter, softened
   2 cups powdered sugar
   1 tsp. vanilla
   2 Tbs. cream, milk or half and half

Combine first four ingredients. Cut butter into flour and salt. Add liquid mixture. Mix well. Divide into two portions, shaping into flat rectangles. Wrap in wax paper or plastic wrap and chill several hours or overnight.
To shape dough, remove one portion from refrigerator. Use a pastry stocking on a rolling pin, if possible. Sprinkle sugar on a board and roll out pastry, adding more sugar as needed to prevent sticking. Move quickly and lightly. Do not handle dough any more than necessary.

Pastry should measure approximately 10x20-inches. Fold into thirds the long way into a 3x20-inch piece. Cut into segments ¾-inch wide. Twist each piece 1½ times. Place on an ungreased cookie sheet. Repeat with other dough section. Put in a warm place to rise for 1 to 1½ hours. Bulk should almost double. Place cookie sheet on middle oven rack. Bake at 375° for 10 to 12 minutes. Remove rolls from baking sheets. Flip upside down to cool.
To make icing, using an electric mixer beat the butter, slowly adding sugar and vanilla. Gradually add the cream. Beat for at least 5 minutes. Glaze the rolls while still slightly warm. Yields 3 dozen.

Gloria Stanford

Breads

Weekend Rolls

You determine the shape of these light and airy rolls.

1 cup milk
½ cup butter
1 tsp. salt
½ cup sugar
1 oz. compressed yeast
2 eggs
4 cups flour

Scald the milk in a 2-quart saucepan. Remove from heat and add butter, salt and sugar. When mixture is lukewarm, crumble in the yeast, add eggs and gradually the flour. Beat thoroughly until the dough bubbles. Put into large mixing bowl and when cooled, cover tightly and refrigerate for 24 hours. When ready to shape, cut in half (or portion desired). Remaining dough can be refrigerated, covered, for a week. Form into rolls. Place in well-greased pans and let rise for several hours. Bake at 375° for 15 minutes. Yield 2 dozen.

Tea rolls:
Roll on a floured board to 1/8-inch thickness a section of dough about 4 inches wide and 12 inches long. Spread with melted butter and a blend of cinnamon sugar. Roll up and cut into 1-inch rolls. Place in pan as described. When baked and cool, frost with vanilla icing.

Tea roll variation:
Roll out wider piece of dough. Spread with butter, cinnamon, sugar, nuts and candied fruits. Roll and place in a ring on a cookie sheet or in a round pan. Make diagonal cut every 2 inches around dough and let rise.

Cloverleaf roll:
Roll dough into 1-inch balls, placing 3 in each section of a muffin tin. Brush tops with melted butter

Twists:
Roll dough ½ inch thick and 7 inches long. Twist one end around other in a rope-like effect. Bake on cookie sheet.

Jean Lindemann

Breads

Lemon Sticky Buns

2¼ to 2¾ cups unsifted flour
¾ cups sugar
1 tsp. salt
1½ tsp. grated lemon peel
1¼-oz. pkg. active dry yeast
⅜ cup milk
¼ cup water
½ stick butter or margarine
1 egg, at room temperature
½ cup chopped, blanched almonds
¼ tsp. ground nutmeg
butter or margarine, melted

In a large bowl, thoroughly mix together ¾ cup flour, ¼ cup sugar, salt, lemon peel and undissolved yeast. Combine milk, water and ½ stick of butter in a saucepan. Heat over low heat until liquids are warm (butter does not need to melt). Gradually add to dry ingredients and beat 2 minutes at medium speed of mixer, scraping bowl occasionally. Add egg and ¼ cup flour or enough flour to make a thick batter. Beat at high speed for 2 minutes, scraping bowl occasionally. Stir in enough additional flour to make a soft dough. Turn out onto a lightly floured board. Knead until smooth and elastic, about 8 to 10 minutes. Place in greased bowl, turning to grease top. Cover and let rise in a warm place free from draft, until doubled in bulk, about 1 hour. Sprinkle chopped almonds into 2 greased 8-inch round cake pans.

Prepare Lemon Topping (below) and pour over almonds.

lemon topping:
Combine ¾ cup sugar, ½ stick butter or margarine, ¼ cup light corn syrup, ⅛ cup water and 1½ Tbs. grated lemon peel in a saucepan. Bring to a boil. Cook 3 minutes, stirring constantly.

Combine remaining ½ cup sugar and nutmeg. Punch dough down. Turn out onto lightly floured board. Divide into 2 equal pieces. Roll each piece into a 15x8-inch rectangle. Brush with melted butter. Sprinkle with sugar and nutmeg mixture. Roll each up from long side as for a jelly roll. Seal edges firmly. Cut into 1-inch slices. Place, cut side up, in prepared pans. Cover and let rise in a warm place, free from draft, until doubled in bulk, about 1 hour. Bake at 350° about 20 to 25 minutes or until done. Invert buns onto plates or wire racks to cool. Yields 2½ dozen.

Marian Miller

Breads

Three Grain Bread

An excellent, tasty bread everyone will love.

3½ cups unbleached flour, divided
1¾ cups medium rye flour
1¾ cups whole-wheat flour
2 tsp. salt
3 ¼-oz. pkgs. dry yeast
1¾ cups milk
¾ cup water
⅔ cup honey
3 Tbs. butter or margarine
2 Tbs. light molasses
½ cup sunflower seeds
¼ cup regular wheat germ
¼ cup millers bran or all bran

In a bowl, combine 2 cups of unbleached flour, rye flour and whole-wheat flour. In a large mixing bowl, combine 3 cups of flour mixture with salt and yeast. In a saucepan over medium-low heat, heat milk, water, honey, margarine and molasses until very warm(120-130°). Add warm liquid to flour mixture. Blend at low speed of mixer until moistened. Beat 3 minutes at medium speed. Stir in sunflower seeds, wheat germ, bran and enough of the remaining 1½ to 2 cups unbleached flour, a little at a time, to make a stiff dough. Turn dough out on a floured surface and knead until smooth and elastic, about 10 minutes. Place dough in greased bowl, turning to grease top. Cover and let rise in warm place until light and doubled in bulk, about 1 hour.

Punch down dough. Divide in half. Let rest, covered with an inverted bowl, 15 minutes. Shape into 2 loaves. Place into 2 well-greased 8½x4½x2½-inch loaf pans. Cover and let rise in warm place until dough fills pans and tops of loaves are about 1 inch above pan edges, about 45 minutes. Bake at 350°, 40 to 45 minutes, until loaves sound hollow when lightly tapped on bottom. To tap, turn loaves out of pan and tap on bottom. If done, return to pans and bake until done. Remove from pans and cool on rack.

Yields 2 loaves

Note: You can use any combination of flours, just so you have the proper total amount.

Gloria Jones

41

Breads

Lighthouse Rye Bread

1½ cups beer
1½ cups sour milk
6 Tbs. sugar
1½ Tbs. salt
1½ Tbs. caraway seed
2 pkgs. dry yeast
3 Tbs. shortening, softened
4½ cups medium rye flour
5 to 6 cups white flour

In a saucepan, combine the beer and milk. Heat to lukewarm, stirring constantly to avoid curdling. Add the sugar, salt, caraway seed and yeast. Stir until dissolved. Add the shortening. Mix well. Combine the rye and white flour. Add enough to the mixture to make a stiff dough. Knead. Let rise in a greased bowl until double in size. Shape into 3 loaves. Place in 3 greased pie tins. Let rise. Bake at 400° for 30 minutes, then at 350° for 25 minutes. Yields 3 loaves.

Carol Tishler

Heidi Muffins

A muffin dough that keeps well for quite a time. Nuts may be added for variety.

3 cups sugar
1 cup butter or margarine, melted
4 eggs, beaten
5 cups flour
5 tsp. baking soda
2 tsp. salt
1 qt. buttermilk
6 cups bran buds
1½ tsp. cinnamon
1 cup raisins

In a very large bowl, mix together the sugar and butter. Add eggs. Mix together the flour, baking soda and salt and add to the sugar mixture. Mix together the buttermilk, bran buds and cinnamon and slowly add to the flour mixture. Add the raisins. Let batter stand in refrigerator overnight. May be refrigerated 1 to 2 weeks, baking as needed or baked at one time and frozen. Fill greased muffin tins and bake at 375° for 20 minutes. Yields 5 dozen.

Bobbe Blumberg

Breads

Wheat Germ Muffins

Delicious served warm or cold. Add raisins for variety.

½ cup wheat germ
½ cup boiling water
½ cup sugar
¼ cup shortening or margarine
1 egg, beaten
1 cup bran flakes or wheat flakes
1¼ cups flour
1¼ tsp. baking soda
¼ tsp. salt
1 cup buttermilk

Put wheat germ in bowl and cover with boiling water. Set aside. Cream sugar and shortening together. Add egg and mix well. Add bran flakes and wheat germ. Sift together the flour, baking soda and salt. Add flour mixture alternately with buttermilk. Fill paper-lined or greased muffin tin ¾ full. Bake at 400° for 20 minutes. May be frozen then wrapped in foil to reheat. Yields 12 muffins.

Carol Dugan

•

Churning butter in colonial times was hard work, yet done by women as well as children. Carrot juice and salt sometimes were added for color and flavor. When the butter was ready, it was scooped into a wooden bowl and worked with paddles to remove the water, then pressed into molds or buckets.

•

Orange-Raisin Muffins

Good to serve warm at breakfast time as they are filling and won't leave you hungry until lunch time. Also good for lunch boxes, busy people and served at a brunch.

¾ cup orange juice
⅓ cup oil
1 egg
1½ cups bite-sized bran cereal
     squares
⅓ cup brown sugar, packed
½ cup raisins or snipped dates
1 cup flour
1½ tsp. baking powder
¼ tsp. salt
½ cup chopped walnuts

Beat together orange juice, oil and egg. Stir in cereal until moistened. Let stand 5 minutes. Stir in brown sugar and raisins. Mix together the flour, baking powder and salt. Add to raisin mixture. Place in greased muffin tins, filling half way. Sprinkle nuts on top. Bake at 400° for 20 minutes or until lightly browned. Sprinkle sugar lightly on top, if desired. Remove immediately from tins. Cool slightly. Yields 1 dozen.

Maggie Schimmel

Breads

Cranberry Muffins

1 egg, beaten
¾ cup milk
2 cups sifted flour
4 tsp. baking powder
¼ cup sugar
½ tsp. salt
4 Tbs. butter or other fat, melted
1 cup cranberries

Combine the beaten egg and milk. Sift together the flour, baking powder, sugar and salt. Add the liquid mixture. Wash cranberries, removing small stems and roll in 2 more tablespoons of sugar. Fold into batter with the melted butter, stirring no more than necessary. Pour into greased muffin tin. Bake at 400° for 30 minutes or until brown. Yields 1 dozen.

Virginia Feind

Sweet Potato Muffins

A nice addition to a Thanksgiving dinner.
½ cup butter, softened
1 cup sugar
1¼ cups cooked, mashed sweet potatoes
2 eggs
2½ cups flour
1½ Tbs. baking powder
½ tsp. cinnamon
1 tsp. nutmeg
1 tsp. salt
1¼ cups milk
½ cup chopped pecans
1½ tsp. lemon extract
¼ cup sugar
1 Tbs. cinnamon

In a bowl, cream together the butter and sugar until light and fluffy. Stir in the sweet potatoes. Add the eggs one at a time, stirring well after each addition. Sift together the flour, baking powder, cinnamon, nutmeg and salt. Stir into the potato mixture alternating with the milk. Stir in the pecans and lemon extract. In a small bowl combine the sugar and cinnamon. Spoon batter into muffin tins, filling ⅔ full. Sprinkle with sugar-cinnamon mixture. Bake at 400° for 25 minutes or until lightly browned. Turn muffins out onto rack. Cool. Yields 2 dozen.

Carol Tishler

Breads

Grigsby's Popovers

Spectacular if baked in old-fashioned, round-bottomed custard cups, as originally intended.

3 eggs
1 cup milk
1 cup flour
1/2 tsp. salt

Mix together all ingredients by hand until just blended. Do not over mix. Fill 10 greased muffin cups 2/3 full. Bake at 450° for 30 minutes. Yield: 10 popovers.

Diane Lane

Yields 10 popovers.

Homemade Baking Powder

Tartrate baking powder is no longer available. Taste connoisseurs are grieving. If you want to avoid the bitter taste of double acting baking powder in delicate recipes such as shortcake and baking powder biscuits, make your own, using one and three fourths times the amount given in a recipe for the double acting baking powder.

2 Tbs. cream of tartar
1 Tbs. baking soda
1 Tbs. corn starch

Sift together the three ingredients. Store in an airtight container.

Sybil La Budde

Cinnamon Puff Balls

1/3 cup butter
1/2 cup sugar
1 egg
1/2 cup sour cream
1 1/2 cups flour
1 1/2 tsp. baking powder
1/2 tsp. salt
1/2 cup raisins, optional
1/2 cup butter, melted
1/2 to 1 cup sugar
2 tsp. cinnamon

Beat together the sugar, butter and egg. Blend in sour cream and dry ingredients. Add raisins and mix well. Fill tiny greased muffin tins 1/2 full. Bake at 375° for 15 minutes. While still warm, dip in melted butter and roll in sugar-cinnamon mixture. Yields 35 puffs.

Bette Schapekahm

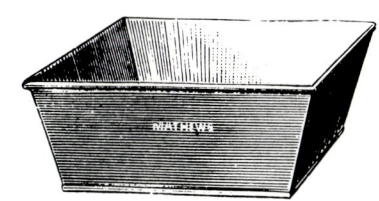

45

Breads

Apple Spice Bread

1⅓ cups all-purpose flour
¾ tsp. baking soda
½ tsp. salt
1 tsp. cinnamon
¼ tsp. ground cloves
1 cup sugar
½ cup oil
2 eggs, beaten
1 tsp. vanilla
2 cups coarsely-chopped apples
½ cup raisins
½ cup chopped nuts
1 tsp. sugar
6 nut halves

Mix together the flour, baking soda, salt, cinnamon and cloves. Set aside. In a large bowl, mix sugar with the oil. Add eggs and vanilla. Stir in apples, raisins and nuts. Add flour mixture. Stir until well mixed. Grease a small-sized bread pan. Line bottom with waxed paper. Pour batter into pan and smooth top. Bake at 325 to 350° for 50 to 60 minutes. After bread has baked 20 minutes, gently pull out oven rack. Sprinkle top with sugar. Place nut halves down the center, pressing slightly. Return rack to oven. Finish baking, testing for doneness with a cake tester. Cool. Yields 1 loaf.

Beverly Jaeger

Zucchini Bread

1 cup oil
3 eggs
2 cups sugar
1½ tsp. nutmeg
1½ tsp. cinnamon
½ tsp. baking soda
½ tsp. baking powder
3 cups flour
2 cups grated zucchini, unpeeled, seeded
½ cup chopped nuts

Beat together the oil, eggs and sugar. Combine the nutmeg, cinnamon, baking soda, baking powder and flour. Blend into sugar mixture. Do not beat. Fold in the zucchini and nuts. Pour into two 9x5-inch loaf pans. Bake at 350° for 1 hour. Yields 2 loaves.

Julie Revane

46

Breads

Peach Kuchen

¼ lb. butter
2 cups flour
¼ tsp. baking powder
¼ tsp. salt
2 Tbs. sugar
5 to 6 fresh peaches, halved or
sliced
½ cup sugar
cinnamon
2 eggs
1 pt. half-and-half cream

Mix butter with flour, baking powder, salt and sugar combined, with a pastry blender or fork. Mixture should be coarse like cornmeal. Pat evenly on bottom and half way up sided of an 8x8-inch glass baking dish. Press firmly. Arrange halves, cut side down, or slices of peaches in pan. Sprinkle with sugar and cinnamon to taste. Bake at 400° for 15 minutes. Remove. Add the eggs which have been slightly blended with the cream. Bake 30 minutes longer. Serve warm or at room temperature. Serve with whipped cream, if you wish. Serves 8 to 10.

Joan Brengel

Perfect Cornbread

Serve hot with lots of butter and honey.

1 cup unbleached white flour
1 cup whole-grain cornmeal, stone-
ground if possible
4 Tbs. sugar
5 tsp. baking powder
¾ tsp. salt
1 egg
1 cup milk
2 Tbs. melted butter

Sift together the dry ingredients. Beat egg with milk. Add to flour mixture along with melted butter. Mix well. Spread batter in a buttered 9-inch pie pan. Bake at 375° for 30 to 35 minutes or until lightly browned around edges. Serves 4 to 6.

Mary Garity

Breads

Fresh Apple and Orange Bread

3 cups sifted flour
1 tsp. baking soda
1½ tsp. baking powder
1 tsp. salt
½ cup shortening
½ cup orange juice
2 eggs
1⅓ cups sugar
1½ apples, cored and sliced
¼ orange, including all of rind
1 cup raisins
½ cup nuts

In a bowl sift together the flour, baking soda, baking powder and salt. Set aside. In a blender put the shortening, juice, eggs and sugar. Blend well. Add the apples and orange. Blend until fruit is chopped fine. Add the raisins and nuts. Blend 15 seconds. Stir in the dry ingredients. Pour into a 9½x5½-inch loaf pan which has been greased and floured. Bake at 350° about 75 minutes or until done. Yields 1 loaf.

Hariette Vick

Irish Soda Bread I

Similar to a baking powder biscuit, this bread toasts well.

5½ cups flour
½ cup sugar
3 tsp. baking powder
½ tsp. baking soda
½ tsp. salt
¼ cup butter
1½ cups currants or raisins
2 cups buttermilk
1 egg

Combine flour, sugar, baking powder, baking soda and salt in a mixing bowl. Cut in butter until mixture is crumbly. Stir in currants. Combine buttermilk and egg. Add to dry ingredients, stirring until blended. Turn out onto a floured board. Knead until smooth. Divide dough in half. Shape into two round loaves. Place on two well-greased baking sheets. Bake at 350° for 45 to 50 minutes. Yields 2 loaves.

Julie Revane

●

A unique feature of American cooking is that women who settled here from other countries brought native recipes with them. Though recipes have been adapted to suit life here, many of our recipes have their origin from the French, Scotch, Irish, Scandinavians, Germans, British, Orientals and Italians.

●

Breads

Irish Soda Bread II

2 cups flour
2 Tbs. sugar
1 tsp. baking powder
1 tsp. baking soda
½ tsp. salt
3 Tbs. butter or margarine, softened
1 cup buttermilk
½ cup seedless raisins, optional
1 Tbs. butter or margarine,
    melted

In a large bowl, sift flour, sugar, baking powder, soda and salt together. Cut in butter with a pastry blender until mixture looks like fine crumbs. Add raisins (optional). Add buttermilk. Mix with a fork only until dry ingredients are moistened. If necessary, sift additional flour over mixture to form a very soft ball. Turn out onto a lightly floured board or pastry cloth. Knead gently until smooth, about 1 minute. Shape into a ball. Place on a lightly greased cookie sheet and flatten into a 7-inch circle about 1½ inches thick. With the tip of a floured knife, cut a ½-inch deep "X" into the dough, dividing the top of the loaf into quarters. Bake at 375° for 30 to 40 minutes. Cool on a wire rack. Brush top with melted butter. Yields 1 loaf.

Carol Tishler

Banana Lemon Bread

Add ½ to 1 cup chopped nuts for added texture, if you wish.

¾ cup butter
2¼ cups sugar
3 eggs
1½ tsp. vanilla
grated rind of 1 lemon
1½ cups mashed bananas, about 3
3 cups flour
1 tsp. baking soda
1 tsp. baking powder
¾ tsp. salt
⅓ cup sour milk or buttermilk

Cream together the butter and sugar. Add the eggs, one at a time, beating well after each addition. Add the vanilla, lemon rind and bananas. Mix well. Sift the dry ingredients together. Add alternately with the milk. Beat well. Turn into 3 well-greased and floured 3½x7½-inch pans. Bake at 350° for 45 minutes, testing for doneness with a cake tester or toothpick. Bread freezes well. Yields 3 small loaves.

Joan Brengel

49

Breads

Easy Herb Dinner Rolls

A simple and very rich roll, dripping with butter.

2 8-oz. pkgs. refrigerated crescent
  rolls
1 cup butter, softened
1/2 cup chopped parsley
1/8 tsp. thyme
sesame seeds

Mix butter, parsley and thyme together. Spread thickly over the bottom of a cookie pan with sides. Remove dough from packages. Slice into ½ -inch rounds (16 per package). Place rounds in pan and sprinkle with sesame seeds. Let stand 1 hour at room temperature. Bake at 375° for 10 to 13 minutes until golden brown. Yields 32 small rolls.

Deborah Holbrook

•

The sesame seed was introduced in America by early African immigrants. Also known as the benne seed, it was a token of good health and good luck.

•

Herb Bread

1 large loaf day-old unsliced bread
1/2 lb. butter, softened
1/4 tsp. each, rosemary, oregano,
  basil and garlic powder or garlic
  salt
1/2 tsp. paprika

Trim crust from top and sides of bread, saving trimmings for bread crumbs. Cut bread into 1-inch slices, cutting to but not through bottom crust. Make one lengthwise cut down the middle of the bread, cutting to but not through bottom crust. Cream together the butter and seasonings. Frost bread mixture, covering top and all sides. Place on a cookie sheet. Bake at 350° for 30 minutes or until brown, basting every 10 minutes. Serve hot or cold. Can be reheated. Serves 8 to 12.

Mitzi Halkerston

Notes

Luncheon and Supper Dishes

Chinese decorative and ceremonial objects

The back row includes a white jadite figurine of two young women beside a flowering tree, of the Chien Lung reign, 1736-1795; a pale green nephrite cup with kylon handles of the Sung dynasty, 960-1279; a white jadite Kwan Yin, the Goddess of Mercy, of the Chia Ching reign 1796-1820; and a wooden three-fold screen inlaid with colored soapstone of the early 20th century. Objects toward the front include a greenish-white nephrite dish of the Sung dynasty, 960-1279; a pair of ivory chopsticks of the Kwang Hsi reign, 1875-1906; and a cloissone dragon of the reign of Chien Lung, 1736-1795.

Luchcheon/Supper Dishes

Hot Tamale Pie

Good on a cold, winter night. Serve with side dishes of sour cream and guacamole.

1½ lbs. lean ground beef
1 onion, chopped
½ cup chopped green pepper
1 tsp. seasoned salt
1 pkg. chili seasoning mix
1 1-lb. can tomatoes
1½ cups cooked, whole-kernel
    corn, drained
1 3¼-oz. can pitted black olives
    (about 1 cup)
1 cup yellow cornmeal
1 tsp. salt
2½ cups cold water
¼ cup chopped, canned pimiento
1 cup shredded cheddar cheese

In a skillet brown meat, breaking up chunks with a fork. Add next 5 ingredients. Simmer 5 minutes. Stir in corn and olives. Combine cornmeal, salt and water in a large saucepan. Cook stirring, until thick. Add pimiento. Stir. Line a greased, shallow, 2-quart baking dish with some of the cornmeal mixture. Pour in beef mixture, making a border of remaining cornmeal around edge of dish. Bake at 350° for 40 minutes. Sprinkle on cheese. Bake 5 minutes longer. Spoon up to serve. Serves 6.

Marie Grayer

Yankee Pastie

pastry for a 2-crust pie
1 lb. ground beef
½ lb. spicy bologna, ground or
    minced
1 cup dry bread crumbs, softened in
    1 cup milk
1 egg
salt and pepper
1 tsp. prepared mustard
¼ cup minced onion

Using your favorite pastry recipe, divide in half. Line a meat loaf pan with half the dough. Mix the remaining ingredients together well. Pack into the loaf pan. Top with remaining dough. Bake at 400° for 1 hour. Slice. Serve hot or cold.
Serves 6 to 8.

Jean Lindemann

Luncheon/Supper Dishes

Dutch Oven Dinner

1 lb. ground beef
1 12-oz. can whole kernel corn, undrained
1 3-oz. can mushroom stems and pieces, undrained
1 29-oz. can tomatoes
1 large onion, sliced
1 green pepper, sliced
1 8-oz. pkg. medium-wide noodles
1 cup diced cheddar cheese
salt and pepper to taste

Brown meat lightly in Dutch oven without added fat. Add remaining ingredients except cheese. Bring to a boil. Cover. Simmer over very low heat for 15 minutes, stirring occasionally. Add cheese. Cover. Simmer 10 to 15 minutes longer, adding a little water if mixture becomes too dry. Salt and pepper to taste. Serves Serves 6.

Marie Grayer

Aunt Sue's Casserole

1 cup elbow macaroni
1 lb. ground chuck
½ cup chopped onion
½ lb. process or cheddar cheese, grated
¼ tsp. oregano
½ tsp. Worcestershire sauce
¼ tsp. hot pepper sauce
1 15-oz. can tomato sauce

Cook macaroni to package directions. Brown meat and onions. Add remaining ingredients and macaroni, mixing well. Place in a casserole. Bake covered at 350° for 45 minutes. Sprinkle with additional grated cheese. Serves 6 to 8.

Sue Wettengel

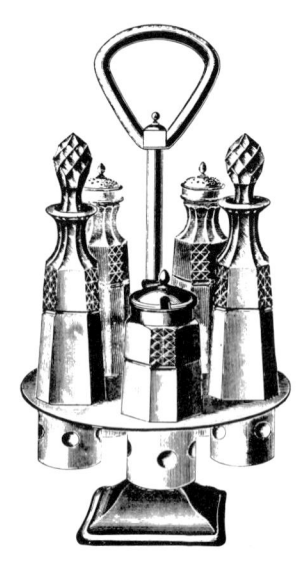

Luncheon/Supper Dishes

Cheeseburger Open Face

Can be made ahead, frozen individually on a cookie sheet, then stored in a plastic bag for a homemade convenience food. Increase baking time if frozen.

1 lb. ground beef
1 cup grated American cheese or chunks of process cheese
1 Tbs. Worcestershire sauce
¼ cup ketchup
1 medium onion, chopped fine
salt and pepper to taste
3 to 6 hamburger buns, halved

Mix together the first 6 ingredients. Spread on buns, covering to edges. Bake at 350° for about 15 minutes. Time will depend on how thickly you spread on the meat mixture and degree of doneness you desire. Serves 4 to 6.

Elizabeth Pleier

"Magic" Meal

This one-dish meal can be served either hot or cold and can be made in advance. Serve with warm garlic bread.

2 lbs. boned chicken breasts
1 lb. fresh mushrooms, sliced
1 cup Italian dressing
½ cup chopped onions
1 Tbs. butter
3 cups sliced zucchini
2 cups cherry tomatoes or 1   1 lb.
  3-oz. can whole tomatoes
½ tsp. salt
½ tsp. hot pepper sauce
½ lb. process cheese, cubed

Bake chicken until tender. Cool. Remove skin and cut into bite-sized pieces. Place chicken pieces and mushrooms in a bowl. Cover with the Italian dressing. Marinate at least 1 hour. In a skillet, cook the onion in butter until slightly brown. Add chicken, mushrooms and marinade. Add zucchini and tomatoes. Cook, stirring constantly, until zucchini is tender. Add the cheese. When melted it is ready to serve. Serves 4 to 6.

Jean Lindemann

Luncheon/Supper Dishes

Chicken Hot Dish

An excellent do-ahead dish for a working cook, for a potluck supper or to take to a sick friend.

1 12-oz. pkg. seasoned bread stuffing
½ stick margarine, melted
1 cup water, chicken broth or chicken bouillon
3 to 4 cups cooked chicken pieces
½ cup mayonnaise
½ cup diced celery
2 eggs
1½ cups milk
1 10-oz. can cream of mushroom soup
½ cup grated sharp cheddar cheese

Mix together bread stuffing, margarine and liquid. Put half in bottom of a buttered casserole or baking dish. Mix together chicken, mayonnaise and celery. Put on top of stuffing. Cover with remaining stuffing mixture. Combine eggs and milk. Beat well. Pour over mixture in casserole dish. Spread with mushroom soup. Sprinkle cheese on top. Refrigerate at least 6 hours or overnight. Bake uncovered at 325° for 1 hour. Serves 6 to 8.

Elizabeth Thier

Peg's Hot Dish for a Crowd

8 lbs. turkey or chicken breasts, cooked, cooled, cut into bite-sized pieces
1½ bunches celery, finely sliced
1½ bunches green onions, using some tops, finely sliced
2 green peppers, finely chopped
3 10-oz. cans cream of chicken soup, undiluted
1 qt. mayonnaise
1 lb. fresh mushrooms, sliced
1 cup slivered almonds (optional)
3 6-oz. cans water chestnuts, drained and sliced
½ cup grated cheddar cheese
½ cup bread crumbs

Mix all ingredients. Place in large casserole or two smaller dishes. Top with cheese which has been mixed with bread crumbs. Bake at 350° for 45 to 60 minutes. Serves 24.

Marie Grayer

Luncheon/Supper Dishes

Chicken and Biscuit Casserole

A good way to use leftover fowl.

2   cups cooked chicken or turkey
1   10-oz. pkg. frozen chopped
    broccoli, cooked and drained
1   10-oz. can cream of chicken soup
1/4   cup chopped onion
1/4   cup sour cream
1 1/2   tsp. Worcestershire sauce
dash of curry
1/4   cup grated cheddar cheese
1   8-oz. can refrigerator biscuits

topping:
  1/4   cup sour cream
  1   egg
  1   tsp. celery seed
  1/2   tsp. salt

Grease a 1 1/2 -qt. casserole. Combine chicken, broccoli, soup, onion, sour cream, Worcestershire sauce and curry. Mix well. Can be refrigerated at this point. Bake at 375° for 20 to 30 minutes, until hot and bubbly. Sprinkle with cheese. Arrange biscuits, which have been cut in half, on top, cut side down. Mix topping ingredients together. Spread over biscuits. Bake for 25 to 30 minutes more or until biscuits are brown. Serves 4 to 6.

Ann Hill

Salmon Mousse

1   16-oz. can salmon
2   envelopes unflavored gelatin
1/2   cup cold water
1   10-oz. can tomato soup,
    undiluted
1   8-oz. pkg. cream cheese, cubed
1   cup mayonnaise
1/3   cup chopped green pepper
1/3   cup grated carrot
4   Tbs. minced onion
juice of 1/2 lemon

Drain and flake salmon. Dissolve gelatin in water. Heat soup. Add cream cheese to soup, stirring until dissolved. Add gelatin and remaining ingredients. Stir with a wisk until smooth. Rinse a mold with cold water. Grease bottom and sides with mayonnaise. Pour in salmon mixture. Refrigerate until set. Use a fish mold if available and serve with a sauce made of sour cream, dill and lemon juice if you wish. Serves 10 to 12.

Ethel Lange

Luncheon/Supper Dishes

Hot Crab Luncheon Dish

1   6-oz. can crabmeat
2   medium zucchini, sliced ¼-inch
    thick
1   small onion, chopped
1   stick butter
2   cloves garlic, crushed
1⅓ cups Swiss cheese, cut into
    strips
3   tomatoes, peeled and coarsely
    chopped
1   cup seasoned bread crumbs
salt and pepper to taste
1   tsp. basil
paprika

In a covered saucepan, saute the
zucchini and onion in ⅔ stick butter
for 12 to 15 minutes. In another pan,
melt remaining butter. Add garlic and
crabmeat. Saute for a few minutes.
Fold into zucchini mixture. Add 1
cup Swiss cheese, tomatoes, ⅔ cup
bread crumbs, salt, pepper and basil.
Mix well. Put into a greased 1½-
quart casserole dish. Sprinkle with
remaining ⅓ cup cheese and ⅓ cup
crumbs. Sprinkle with paprika. Bake
at 375° for 30 to 40 minutes.
Serves 6.

Judy Heiligenstein

Curried Tuna Casserole

12 oz. thin spaghetti or linguini,
    broken into 4-inch lengths
4   7-oz. cans solid packed tuna in
    water, drained and flaked
2   10-oz. cans cream of mushroom
    soup
1   14-oz. can chicken broth
2   chicken bouillon cubes
1   8-oz. can mushroom stems and
    pieces
1   to 2 tsp. curry or to taste
½   tsp. thyme
¼   tsp. basil
¼   tsp. oregano
1   Tbs. grated onion
½   cup dry bread crumbs
3   Tbs. butter, melted

Cook spaghetti al dente according to
package directions. Drain. In a
saucepan, blend together the mushroom soup and chicken broth. Add
the bouillon cubes. Cook over
medium heat until cubes are dissolved. Moisten curry with a small
amount of mushroom liquid. Add
curry, mushrooms plus liquid,
thyme, basil, oregano and onion to
soup mixture. Correct seasonings.
Combine tuna, spaghetti and soup
mixture. Toss lightly. Pour into a
buttered 9x13-inch casserole. Combine crumbs with butter. Sprinkle
over top. Bake at 350° for 1 hour or
until bubbly and lightly browned.
Serves 10 to 12.

Jeanette Oberndorfer

Luncheon/Supper Dishes

Jambalaya Casserole

An easy casserole to prepare ahead. Serve with a tossed vegetable salad or marinated vegetable platter and hot French bread for a New Orleans Creole type meal.

1 cup onion, diced
1 cup green pepper, seeded and diced
1 large clove garlic, minced
2 cups uncooked rice
2 tsp. salt
⅛ tsp. cayenne pepper
1 tsp. Worcestershire sauce
1 16-oz. can tomatoes
1½ lbs. shelled, deveined shrimp, fresh or frozen (thawed enough to separate)
1 lb. ham, diced
3½ cups boiling water
2 bay leaves

Saute onion, green pepper and garlic in bacon drippings until soft. Stir in rice, seasonings, tomatoes, shrimp and ham. Place in a 3-quart casserole. Cover. Refrigerate until cooking time. When ready to cook, pour boiling water over. Place bay leaves near top where they can be removed easily. Bake at 350° for 1 hour or until rice is tender. Remove bay leaves. Fluff up the top with a fork. Garnish with cooked bacon bits if desired. Serves 8.

Sybil La Budde

Meatless Main Dish

As a snack, serve cold without the sauce, cut into squares.

4 eggs, beaten
1 lb. cheddar cheese, coarsely shredded
1½ cups chopped walnuts
1 cup cooked rice
½ cup quick rolled oats
½ cup finely chopped mushrooms
1 onion, minced
garlic salt
¼ tsp. salt
¼ tsp. pepper

mushroom sauce:
⅓ cup butter
3 Tbs. flour
2 cups milk
¼ tsp. salt
⅛ tsp. pepper
1 lb. fresh mushrooms, sliced

Blend together all the ingredients except the sauce. Pack firmly into a well-greased 9x5x3-inch loaf pan. Bake at 350° for 50 minutes. To make sauce, melt butter. Blend flour. Slowly add the milk, salt and pepper. Cook gently for 5 minutes. Add the mushrooms. Heat slightly. When loaf is cooked, loosen and turn out onto a warm serving dish. Serve with the hot mushroom sauce. Serves 6.

Jean Lindemann

Luncheon/Supper Dishes

Mexican Pancake

8 eggs
1 cup flour
2 cups skim milk
1 tsp. salt
2 Tbs. butter
2 Tbs. oil
1 onion, thinly sliced
1 can green chilies, chopped
4 oz. pkg. cream cheese, cubed
½ can pitted black olives, sliced

salsa:
    4 tomatoes, peeled, seeded,
    chopped
    1 can jalapeno chilies, chopped
    3 green onions, minced
    ½ bunch cilantro, chopped or ½
    to 1 tsp. dried
    salt to taste

Preheat oven to 500°. Beat eggs, flour, milk and salt together to make a batter. Place oil and butter in a baking dish. Place in oven. When oil sizzles, add onion and chilies. Saute 2 to 3 minutes. Add cheese and olives. Pour on batter. Bake 12 minutes or until pancake puffs. Lower heat to 375°. Bake 15 minutes more. To make salsa, blend together all ingredients but do not puree. There should be some texture. Serve cold or at room temperature with the pancake. Serves 4 to 6.

Elizabeth Pleier

Mother's German Pancake

3 large or 4 small eggs
pinch of salt
1 Tbs. sugar
½ cup milk
½ cup flour
2 Tbs. butter

filling:
    2 or 3 peaches or apples, sliced
    ¾ cup sugar
    ¼ cup butter
    1 Tbs. lemon juice
    ¼ tsp. cinnamon

Beat eggs. Add salt and sugar. Beat again. Add milk and flour. Beat until well mixed. Pour into a cold, buttered 9 or 10-inch oven-proof skillet. Bake at 400° until it puffs up and browns, about 15 minutes. Reduce heat to 375°. Bake another 5 to 10 minutes. Meanwhile, combine filling ingredients in a saucepan. Cook gently for about 5 minutes. Spread over cooked pancake and fold in half. Serves 2.

Julie Revane

Luncheon/Supper Dishes

Chicken-Zucchini Flips

¼ cup chopped onion
¼ cup thinly sliced celery
2 Tbs. butter or margarine
1 10 ¾-oz. can cream of chicken
  soup
¼ cup milk
salt and pepper to taste
¼ cup white wine, optional
2 cups diced, cooked chicken
2 eggs, beaten
¼ cup all-purpose flour
2 Tbs. grated parmesan cheese
1 tsp. each chopped parsley and
  chives
3 medium zucchini, about 2 cups,
  shredded and drained

In a small saucepan, cook onion and celery in butter until soft but not brown. Add soup, milk, salt, pepper and wine, if you wish. Stir in chicken. Heat through. Keep warm. In a medium bowl, combine eggs, flour, cheese, chives, parsley, salt and pepper. Add zucchini. Mix well. Drop ¼ cup of zucchini mixture on a heated, greased griddle or into a skillet. Pat quite thin. Cook until browned on one side and mixture is partially set. Turn and brown other side. Remove and keep warm. Repeat until you have 8 pancakes. Spoon chicken filling on one half of a pancake. Fold over and add more filling on top, dividing for 8 pancakes. Serves 8.

Peg Nelson

Scallion Gougere

For a light supper serve these hot with a soup and salad.

6 Tbs. butter
½ cup thinly sliced scallions, white
  part only
1 cup water
1 tsp. salt
⅛ tsp. pepper
1 cup flour
4 large eggs
½ cup grated Swiss cheese
1 tsp. Dijon mustard
¼ tsp. dry mustard
1 Tbs. minced chives
¼ cup grated cheddar cheese

Simmer butter and scallions in a saucepan for 2 to 3 minutes. Add water, salt and pepper. Bring to a boil. Immediately stir in the flour, stirring until it forms a ball. With a mixer, beat in the eggs, one at a time. Stir in Swiss cheese, both mustards and chives. Lightly grease and flour a small baking sheet or 12-inch pie plate. Spoon mixture onto baking sheet to form a 10 to 12-inch ring. Spoonfuls should touch. Sprinkle with cheddar cheese. Bake at 425° for 40 to 50 minutes, until puffed and golden. Cut a few slits in top to keep from getting soggy. Serves 6 to 8.

Nina Hayssen

Luncheon/Supper Dishes

Spaghetti Sauce

1¼ lbs. ground beef
3½ cups tomatoes
2 6-oz. cans tomato paste
¼ cup chopped onion
1 clove garlic, minced
2 Tbs. chopped parsley
1 cup water
1½ tsp. salt
½ tsp. pepper
½ Tbs. sugar
1 bay leaf
1½ tsp. oregano

Brown meat in small amount of hot fat in Dutch oven. Add remaining ingredients. Simmer uncovered (do not boil), stirring occasionally, for 1½ hours. Serve over hot, cooked spaghetti, and top with Parmesan cheese. Makes 6 to 8 servings.

Marian Miller

Spicy Zucchini Souffle

8 oz. bulk Italian sausage
4 medium (1½ lbs.) zucchini
½ cup grated parmesan or romano cheese
½ cup fine dry bread crumbs
1 Tbs. snipped fresh parsley
½ tsp. oregano
½ tsp. basil
½ tsp. salt
pinch of freshly ground pepper
3 eggs, separated
2 Tbs. water
paprika

Brown sausage. Drain off fat. Remove ends from zucchini. Cook in small amount of boiling water until tender crisp, about 8 minutes. Drain. Cut off 3 or 4 thin slices for garnish. Set aside. Finely chop or grate remaining zucchini. In a large bowl, combine cheese and bread crumbs, reserving 2 tablespoons for topping. To remaining crumbs, add sausage, chopped zucchini, parsley, herbs, salt and pepper. Toss together. Beat egg yolks and water until blended. Stir into sausage mixture. Wash beaters. Beat egg whites to stiff peaks. Fold into sausage mixture. Turn into an ungreased 1½-quart casserole or souffle dish. Sprinkle with reserved crumb mixture and paprika. Bake, uncovered, at 325° for 50 minutes or until set. Garnish with zucchini slices. Serves 4.

Mary Garity

Luncheon/Supper Dishes

Italian Beef and Green Noodles

Make this casserole the day before serving to develop flavors.

1   8-oz. pkg. green noodles
¼   cup butter or margarine
¼   cup grated parmesan cheese
2   Tbs. olive or salad oil
1   cup chopped onion
2   cloves garlic, crushed
1½ lbs. ground chuck
½   cup water
2   Tbs. dry sherry
1   Tbs. Worcestershire sauce
2   beef bouillon cubes or 2 pkgs. instant
1   tsp. salt
¼   tsp. pepper
2   cups grated gouda, mozarella or American process cheese, divided
¼   cup pine nuts or slivered almonds
¼   cup chopped pimiento

Cook and drain noodles according to package directions. Turn into a bowl and toss with butter and parmesan cheese. Place in a 9x13-inch baking dish, mounding higher around edges. Cover with plastic wrap. Set aside. Saute onion and garlic in oil until golden. Add ground chuck. Brown over medium heat, breaking up with a fork. Reduce heat. Add water, sherry, Worcestershire, bouillon, salt and pepper. Cook until bouillon is dissolved, about 5 minutes. Add 1½ cups of cheese and remaining ingredients. Cook until cheese is melted. Correct seasonings. Pour into noodle-lined dish. Sprinkle on remaining cheese. Cover loosely with foil. Bake at 350° for 20 to 25 minutes, or until hot and cheese is melted. Serves 6.

Jeanette Oberndorfer

Luncheon/Supper Dishes

Neopolitan Casserole

1/4 cup salad or olive oil
1/3 cup finely chopped onion
3 cloves garlic, crushed
1 cup diced carrots
1 1/2 cups diced celery
1 1/2 lbs. ground chuck
1 6-oz. can mushroom caps,
    drained
1/2 cup sherry wine
1 6-oz. can tomato paste
1 1 lb. 3-oz. can tomatoes
1 Tbs. salt or to taste
1/2 tsp. pepper
1/2 tsp. oregano
1/2 tsp. basil
1 10-oz. pkg. frozen, chopped
    spinach, thawed and squeezed dry
1 8-oz. pkg. small shell macaroni,
    cooked and drained
1/2 to 1 cup fresh bread cubes,
    buttered
1 cup grated sharp cheddar
grated parmesan cheese

Heat oil in a skillet. Add onion, garlic, carrot and celery. Saute until golden. Add meat. Cook, stirring constantly until red disappears. Add mushrooms, sherry, tomato paste, tomatoes and seasonings. Simmer uncovered for 1 1/2 hours. Add more seasonings if you wish. Cool, cover and refrigerate until serving time. When ready to cook, reheat sauce and add the macaroni shells and spinach. Turn into a 3-quart casserole. Sprinkle on the bread cubes and cheddar. Bake uncovered at 350° for 30 minutes or until bubbly and brown. Sprinkle with parmesan cheese. Serves 6 to 8.

Jeanette Oberndorfer

Luncheon/Supper Dishes

Lasagna

1 lb. ground beef
3 cloves garlic, minced
1 lb. Italian sausage, crumbled
1 8-oz. can tomato sauce
1 16-oz. can Italian tomatoes
½ tsp. pepper
1 tsp. oregano
½ lb. lasagna noodles
2 tsp. salt
1 Tbs. cooking oil
1 8-oz. pkg. mozzarella cheese
1 16-oz. carton small curd cottage
  cheese
2 eggs
parmesan cheese

Brown beef, garlic and Italian sausage. Drain grease. Blend in tomato sauce, tomatoes, pepper and oregano. Simmer 1 hour or until thick. Cook lasagna noodles in boiling water with salt and oil. Drain. Arrange half of noodles in a 9x12-inch pan. Top with half of mozzarella slices. Combine cottage cheese with eggs, blending well. Spoon half of cottage cheese mixture on mozzarella. Add half of ground beef/tomato mixture. Sprinkle with parmesan cheese. Repeat layer. Bake at 375° for 30 minutes. Can be made ahead of time and frozen before cooking. Serves 6 to 8.

Beverly Quirk

Raggedy Beef

4 to 5 lbs. boneless rump roast
2½ beef bouillon cubes
1½ cups water
½ pkg. dry onion soup mix
hamburger buns

Heat bouillon cubes, water and soup mix to boiling. Place meat in a Dutch oven or baking dish. Pour soup mix over meat. Cover tightly. Bake at 325° for 6 hours. Check halfway through cooking time. Add more water and bouillon if necessary. Take meat out of juice. Shred or break apart with a knife and fork. Return meat to juice. Refrigerate covered overnight. Reheat to serve. Serve on buns. Serves 15-20.

Marian Miller

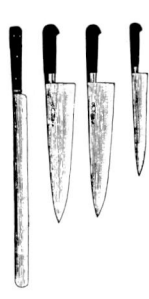

Luncheon/Supper Dishes

Mexican Lasagna

2 lbs. ground beef
1 large onion, chopped
1 to 2 cloves garlic, minced
⅛ cup chili powder (more
   for a spicier dish)
3 cups tomato sauce
½ tsp. sugar
1 cup pitted black olives, sliced
1 4-oz. can whole green chilies,
   chopped
12 corn tortillas, lightly fried in a
   little oil
2 cups small-curd cottage cheese or
   ricotta
1 egg
½ lb. Monterey Jack cheese, sliced
1 cup grated cheddar cheese
½ cup chopped green onions
1 cup sour cream

Brown meat, onion and garlic. Do not let garlic burn. Add chili powder, tomato sauce, sugar, ½ cup of chopped olives and chilies. Simmer 15 minutes. Cut tortillas into quarters. Beat together the cottage cheese and egg. In a 10x14x4-inch baking dish, spread one-third of meat mixture. Cover with half of Jack cheese, half of cottage cheese mixture and half of tortillas. Repeat layers, ending with last one-third of meat mixture. Top with cheddar cheese. Bake at 350° for 30 minutes or until heated through and bubbly. Combine remaining chopped olives, chopped onions and sour cream. Serve as a garnish. Dish may be prepared ahead and refrigerated. Bring to room temperature before baking. Serves 8.

Elizabeth Pleier

•

The first successful canned convenience food was baked beans in tomato sauce. Canned corn also was an early success.

•

Luncheon/Supper Dishes

Casserole Mexicana

1 Tbs. oil
1½ lbs. ground beef
1 envelope chili or sloppy Joe seasoning mix
1 20-oz. can kidney beans
1 8-oz. can tomato sauce
1 4½-oz. can chopped, pitted black olives, drained
1 6-oz. pkg. tortilla chips
½ to 1 cup grated cheddar cheese

Heat oil in a large skillet. Brown beef. Stir in seasoning mix, undrained kidney beans and tomato sauce. Bring to a boil, stirring constantly. Put meat mixture into a 2-quart casserole. Sprinkle on olives. Arrange half of chips around edges. Sprinkle cheese on chips. Bake at 350° for 10 minutes or until cheese is melted. Place remaining chips in a basket to serve with casserole. Serves 6.

Tish Kerchner

Ground Beef and Noodle Casserole

1 lb. ground beef
½ cup chopped onion
½ cup milk
1 10-oz. can cream of celery soup
½ tsp. salt
½ tsp. fresh ground pepper
¼ tsp. thyme
2 to 3 cups cooked medium-wide noodles
1 8-oz. pkg. shredded sharp cheddar cheese

Brown meat. Add onion. Cook until tender. Stir in soup, milk and seasonings. Layer half of noodles, half of meat mixture and half of cheese in a 1½-qt. casserole. Repeat layers of noodles and meat. Bake at 350° for 20 minutes. Add remaining cheese. Bake 10 minutes more. Can be made ahead and cooked just before serving time. Serves 4 to 5.

Gloria Mitchelson

69

Luncheon/Supper Dishes

Eggplant Casserole

4 cups peeled and sliced eggplant
4 cups sliced fresh mushrooms
2 cups peeled and chopped
   tomatoes
¾ cup chopped green onions
¼ cup minced parsley
½ tsp. minced garlic
salt, pepper, oregano and basil to
   taste
1 cup shredded sharp cheddar
   cheese

In a casserole dish put a layer of eggplant. Season with salt, pepper, oregano and sprinkle on half of the green onions. Add a layer of mushrooms. Season with salt, pepper and add the parsley and minced garlic. Add a layer of tomatoes. Season with salt, pepper, basil and add remaining green onions. Bake covered at 350° for 25 minutes. Add the cheese. Cook until the cheese is melted. Serves 6 to 8.

Florence Fitzgerald

Herbed Spinach Bake

1 10-oz. pkg. frozen chopped
   spinach, cooked and drained
1 cup cooked white rice
1 cup shredded American cheese
2 eggs, slightly beaten
2 Tbs. butter or margarine
⅓ cup milk
½ to 1 tsp. salt
¼ tsp. crushed rosemary
¼ tsp. crushed oregano

Mix all ingredients together and pour into 10x6x1½-inch baking dish. Bake at 350° for 20 to 25 minutes, or until inserted knife comes out clean. Cut in squares to serve. Serves 6.

Mildred Booth

Luncheon/Supper Dishes

Fettucini and Spinach

1 8-oz. pkg. fettucini noodles,
   cooked and drained
1 10-oz. pkg. frozen chopped
   spinach, thawed, drained,
   squeezed dry
1 clove garlic, finely chopped
¼ cup oil
1 tsp. dry bouillon
½ cup water
½ tsp. basil
1 cup small-curd cottage cheese
½ tsp. salt
¼ cup grated cheese (parmesan,
   romano or other)
1 tsp. chopped parsley

In a large skillet, cook spinach and garlic in oil for 5 minutes, stirring frequently. Dissolve bouillon in water. Add to spinach. Add basil, cottage cheese and salt. Stir over low heat until blended. Toss together the spinach mixture, grated cheese and noodles. Serve in a heated dish. Garnish with parsley. Serves 4 to 6.

Julie Revane

Corn Chili Strata

A main-meal dish that will delight any vegetarian.

6 slices whole-wheat bread
1 to 1½ Tbs. butter
1 16-oz. can corn, drained
2 cups thinly sliced zucchini
1 14-oz. can green chili peppers,
   diced
8 oz. shredded Jack cheese
4 eggs
2 cups milk
½ tsp. salt
⅛ tsp. pepper

Lightly spread bread slices with butter. Fit into a lightly-greased 7x11-inch baking dish. Pour corn over bread. Then add layers of zucchini, chili peppers and cheese. Beat eggs slightly. Add milk, salt and pepper. Pour over cheese. Cover and refrigerate several hours. Bake at 375° for 30 to 40 minutes. Let stand 10 minutes before serving. Serves 6 to 8.

Carol Dickson

Luncheon/Supper Dishes

Spinach Casserole

A good vegetarian main dish—use as filling to make a quiche.

3 cups cooked rice
2 10-oz. pkgs. frozen spinach, cooked and drained
5 eggs, beaten
2/3 cup milk
1/4 cup melted butter
1/2 cup minced onion
2 tsp. parsley flakes or 2 Tbs. fresh chopped parsley
1 tsp. Worcestershire sauce
1/2 tsp. nutmeg
2 cups grated sharp cheddar cheese
2 cans frozen shrimp soup, defrosted or 1 can small shrimp and 1 10½-oz. can cream of mushroom soup

Combine all ingredients. Place in a large buttered casserole. Bake at 325° for 1 hour. Serves 10 to 12.

Helen Streich

Cheese Strata for Twelve

12 slices white sandwich bread
3/4 lb. sharp cheddar cheese, sliced
1 10-oz. pkg. frozen broccoli, cooked and drained
2 cups diced, cooked ham
6 eggs, slightly beaten
3½ cups milk
1 tsp. salt
1/4 tsp. dry mustard
dash or two Worcestershire sauce
grated cheese

Cut 12 rounds from bread slices. Set aside. Arrange scraps in a large, greased baking dish. Place cheese slices on top. Add a layer of broccoli, then one of ham. Arrange circles of bread on top. Mix together the remaining ingredients except grated cheese. Pour over all. Cover. Refrigerate overnight. Bake uncovered at 325° for 55 minutes. Sprinkle with grated cheese. Bake 5 minutes longer. Let stand 10 minutes before serving. If making half of recipe, use an 8x8-inch square pan. Serves 12.

Marie Grayer

Luncheon/Supper Dishes

Cheese Souffle

Serve with ham, sausage or bacon. This make-ahead dish would be good to serve to weekend house guests.

4 slices bread, diced
¾ lb. sharp cheddar cheese, grated
4 eggs, beaten
2 cups milk
½ tsp. salt
¼ tsp. dry mustard
2 Tbs. sherry

Layer bread and cheese in a 9x12-inch greased baking dish. Combine remaining ingredients. Mix well. Pour over bread-cheese mixture. Refrigerate overnight for breakfast, brunch or lunch. Set dish in a pan of water (1 or 2 inches). Bake at 350° for 50 to 60 minutes. Remove dish from water a few minutes before baking time is complete to make certain bottom is set. Serves 4.

Leitzel Malzahn

Puffy Omelet

Fillings, such as chopped mushrooms, chopped ham, or tomatoes, may be added if desired.

4 eggs, separated
½ cup mayonnaise
3 Tbs. water
2 Tbs. butter or margarine
1 cup shredded sharp cheddar cheese
2 tsp. French tarragon or fresh snipped chives

Beat egg whites until soft peaks form. Combine egg yolks, mayonnaise and water. Mix well. Fold into egg whites. Melt butter over low heat in an oven-proof omelet pan. Cook over medium-low heat for 10 minutes or until lightly browned on bottom but still moist on top. Bake at 350° for 5 minutes. Sprinkle cheese and herbs on top. Bake 1 to 2 minutes more. Remove from oven. Make a shallow cut down center and fold in half. Serves 2.

Mary Garity

Luncheon/Supper Dishes

Scrambled Eggs with Carrots

Good for a light Sunday night supper or luncheon.

5 Tbs. butter
¾ cup ½-inch square bread cubes
6 eggs, beaten
6 Tbs. milk
½ tsp. salt
¾ cup finely grated carrots

Melt 4 tablespoons butter in a skillet. Add bread cubes. Saute on all sides until golden. Remove from skillet. Melt remaining 1 tablespoon of butter. Mix eggs, milk, salt, carrots and browned bread cubes together. Pour into skillet. Cook slowly over low heat, stirring to prevent sticking, until eggs are set. Serves 4.

Mary-Test Lloyd-Jones

Spring Scrambled Eggs

Serve with crisp bacon, hot rolls or muffins and fresh fruit for a brunch that guests will rave about.

9 eggs, lightly beaten
2 to 3 Tbs. butter
5 or 6 green onions, chopped
2 tomatoes, peeled, seeded and diced
¼ cup minced parsley
5 or 6 pitted ripe olives, sliced (do not use canned chopped olives)

Saute onions in butter until translucent. Add tomato. Cook for 3 to 4 minutes. Add eggs. Stir gently with fork or slotted spoon to scramble. When eggs begin to set, add parsley and olives. Serves 6.

Elizabeth Pleier

Luncheon/Supper Dishes

Zucchini Pie

For easier preparation, substitute a prepared pie shell. For variety, other vegetables can be added or substituted for the zucchini.

4 cups thinly sliced zucchini
1 cup chopped onion
½ cup margarine
½ cup chopped parsley
½ tsp. salt
½ tsp. black pepper
¼ tsp. garlic powder
¼ tsp. basil
¼ tsp. oregano
2 eggs, well beaten
8 oz. mozzarella or muenster cheese, shredded
1 8-oz. can refrigerated crescent rolls
2 tsp. Dijon mustard

In a 10-inch skillet, cook zucchini and onion in margarine until tender, about 10 minutes. Stir in the seasonings. Blend the eggs with the cheese. Stir into vegetable mixture. Separate the dough into 8 triangles. Place in an ungreased 10-inch pie pan, 11-inch quiche pan or 12x8-inch baking pan. Press over bottom and up sides. Spread mustard over dough. Pour in vegetable mixture. Bake at 375° for 18 to 20 minutes. If crust becomes too brown, cover with foil the last 10 minutes of baking time. Let stand 10 minutes before serving. Cut into small wedges. Can be frozen before baking time. If frozen, bake for 50 minutes. Yields 8 to 10 slices.

Bobbe Blumberg

Luncheon/Supper Dishes

Salmon Quiche

Can be chilled and served cold for picnics.

1 deep-dish frozen pie crust
prepared mustard
¼ cup minced onions
1 large can salmon, flaked
1 cup grated cheddar cheese
2 eggs, slightly beaten
2 egg yolks, slightly beaten
1½ cups cream
½ tsp. basil
½ tsp. oregano
salt and pepper

Bake frozen pie crust at 400° for 15 minutes. Brush with prepared mustard to seal. Return to oven. Bake 2 minutes more. Layer onions, then salmon, then cheese into baked crust. Combine remaining ingredients together. Mix well. Pour over salmon mixture. Bake at 350° for 35 to 45 minutes. Do not overbake or custard will become watery. Center should shake slightly when done. Cool 10 minutes before slicing. Serves 6.

Nina Hayssen

Swiss Cheese Pie

A different kind of quiche to serve either as an appetizer or light supper dish.

2 9½-oz. pkgs. pie crust mix
1 egg white, slightly beaten
1 lb. Swiss gruyere cheese, grated
1 cup thinly sliced green onions with tops
6 eggs, slightly beaten
2 cups whipping cream
1 cup half-and-half
½ cup dry white wine
1 tsp. salt
½ tsp. each of nutmeg, dry mustard, pepper

Prepare pie crust according to package directions. Roll out to line bottom and sides of a 15x10x1-inch jelly roll pan. Brush with a little egg white. Sprinkle on cheese. Top with onions. Mix remaining ingredients together. Pour gently into shell. Bake at 400° for 35 to 40 minutes or until custard is set. Cut into 60 small squares for an appetizer or 15 squares to serve as a supper dish. Dish may be cut in half. Bake in a 13x9-inch pan at 400° for 35 to 40 minutes. Yields 60 squares.

Carol Dickson

Luncheon/Supper Dishes

Salmon Pie

1   10-inch pie shell, partially baked
     for 5 minutes
1   14-oz. can of salmon, drained
juice of ½ a lemon
2   Tbs. butter
½   cup chopped onion
3   Tbs. chopped parsley
5   eggs
1¼ cups half and half or milk
1   tsp. seasoned salt
pepper

Flake salmon into pie shell. Drizzle lemon over. Melt butter in a small frying pan. Saute onion until limp. Add parsley and pour over salmon. Beat eggs, milk and seasonings together. Pour over salmon. Bake at 350° about 50 minutes or until set. Let rest for 10 minutes before serving. This recipe will not freeze well but reheats nicely. Serves 6.

Diane Wright

Ted's Southern Style Chili

This version is not a soup style dish but is served as a hot meat with beans——typical to Southerners.

2   to 2½ lbs. ground beef
4   Tbs. chili powder
1   tsp. ground cuminseed
2   small cans tomato sauce
dark red kidney beans

Saute meat in a skillet, breaking up into small pieces with no large lumps, until done but not overly brown. Do not allow to get hard. Add chili powder, cuminseed and tomato sauce. Simmer on low for 1 to 1½ hours. Serve with heated dark red kidney beans. Serves 4 to 6.

Marie Grayer

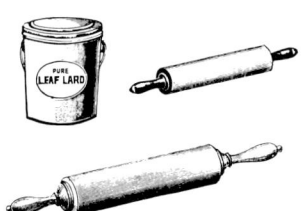

Luncheon/Supper Dishes

Super Chili

A very spicy standard. Serve with corn muffins or French bread or add cooked macaroni for a heartier dish.

2 lbs. ground sirloin or chuck
1 large onion, chopped
1 garlic clove, minced
1 8-oz. can tomato sauce
1 10¾-oz. can tomato soup, undiluted
1 cup water
3 Tbs. chili powder
salt and pepper to taste
1 Tbs. paprika
¼ tsp. each cumin and cayenne pepper

Brown meat. Add onion and garlic. Cook until onion is soft, being careful not to burn garlic. Add remaining ingredients. Cover and simmer for 1 hour. Remove cover and simmer to remove excess moisture. Do not allow to get too dry. Serves 6 to 8

Elizabeth Pleier

Luncheon Crabmeat Sandwich

1 8-oz. pkg. cream cheese, softened
1 Tbs. mayonnaise
1 tsp. Worcestershire sauce
1 Tbs. minced chives or green onions
1 tsp. lemon juice
½ tsp. salt
1 7½-oz. can crabmeat, drained and flaked
8 Holland rusks or 4 English muffins, split
8 thin tomato slices
mayonnaise
8 slices of American cheese

Combine all ingredients through crabmeat. Mix well. Spread evenly on rusk. Top each with a tomato slice. Spread with mayonnaise. Top each with a slice of cheese. Bake at 325° for 15 minutes. Serve immediately. Serves 8.

Bette Schapekahm

Notes

Entrees

Korean greyish-black stoneware of the Old Silla and Silla time period,
5th to 10th century A.D.

In the back row is a small bottle and two large cooking vessels with incised
designs. In the front row is a cup in the form of a man in a leather boat, a
ewer in the shape of a mounted horseman in full armour, and a dragon-shaped
wine ewer. The spreading feet on most of the vessels have triangular or
rectangular openings because the pieces were placed over charcoal for
heating the contents.

Entrees: Meat

Skillet Beef

Serve over hot rice with soy sauce on the side.

1 lb. lean beef, cut into very thin
   strips
2 Tbs. vegetable oil
1 cup sliced celery
1 medium onion, sliced
1 cup diagonally-sliced fresh green
   beans
1 cup green pepper, sliced into
   strips
½ of 8-oz. can water chestnuts,
   drained and sliced
1 14-oz. can bean sprouts, drained
4 tsp. cornstarch
1 Tbs. soy sauce
¾ cup water
4 oz. fresh mushrooms, sliced
salt

In a skillet, brown meat in oil. Add vegetables, water chestnuts and sprouts. Cook 5 to 6 minutes longer. Combine the cornstarch, soy sauce and water. Add to meat mixture, stirring well. Add mushrooms. Cook 10 minutes, stirring until liquid is clear and shiny and beans are tender. Salt to taste. Serves 6 to 8.

Peg Nelson

Beef Stroganoff with Tomato Soup

A variation using a more economical cut of beef. Flavor improves if made a day ahead.

1 lb. round steak, cut in ¾-inch
   pieces
¼ cup flour
2 Tbs. cooking oil
½ cup chopped onion
1 clove garlic, minced
1 6-oz. can broiled mushrooms
1 cup sour cream
1 10¾-oz. can tomato soup
1 Tbs. Worcestershire sauce
6 to 8 drops hot pepper sauce
½ tsp. salt
⅛ tsp. pepper
¼ tsp. marjoram
¼ tsp. rosemary
¼ tsp. basil
¼ tsp. thyme

Dredge meat in flour. Place oil in skillet. Add meat, garlic and onion. Brown meat over medium heat, about 10 minutes. Add mushrooms with liquid. Combine with rest of ingredients except sour cream. Cover tightly. Simmer until tender, about 1½ hours. Cool. Then add sour cream. Reheat. Serve over noodles or rice. Serves 4 to 5.

Sue Wettengel

Entrees: Meat

Chinese Steak Strips with Lettuce

The second marinade recipe should be used for a more authentic Chinese flavor.

¾ lb. sirloin tip, flank or bottom round steak
marinade:
   2 tsp. sugar
   1 Tbs. cornstarch
   2 tsp. vinegar
   1 Tbs. soy sauce
   ½ tsp. salt
   ¼ tsp. pepper
3 slices bacon, diced
3 green onions, thinly sliced, separating white from green
1 head of lettuce (butter, romaine, leaf or iceberg), cut crosswise into ½-inch thick slices
3 thin slices lemon with peel, cut in half (optional)
3 Tbs. oil
cooked rice or Chinese noodles, heated

Thinly slice meat across the grain into 1/8-inch thick strips. Add to marinade. Coat well. Marinate at least 30 minutes, preferably longer. Cook bacon until crisp. Drain well.

Heat oil (bacon drippings may be used, if you wish) until very hot in a wok or electric fry pan (375°). Add steak with marinade. Cook, stirring until meat has changed color. Remove from pan. Add lettuce, white part of onions and lemon slices. Cook, tossing, for 1 minute, until lettuce just starts to wilt. Return steak to pan. Add bacon. Stir well. Garnish with green onion tops. Serves 3 to 4.

alternate marinade:
   ¼ tsp. monosodium glutamate
   ¼ tsp. baking soda
   ¼ tsp. sugar
   dash white pepper
   1 tsp. cornstarch
   1 tsp. oyster sauce
   1 tsp. soy sauce
   1 tsp. peanut oil
   ¼ tsp. sesame oil
   ¼ tsp. salt
   ¼ egg white
   2 Tbs. dry sherry

Ann Hill

84

Entrees: Meat

Beef Bavarian

1½ lbs. *beef round steak, thinly sliced*
4 Tbs. *cornstarch*
2 tsp. *salt*
¼ tsp. *pepper*
¼ tsp. *garlic powder*
2 Tbs. *vegetable oil*
1 *large onion, sliced*
1 *12-oz. can beer*
1 *cup beef broth*
¼ tsp. *hot pepper sauce*
1 Tbs. *brown sugar*
4 *large carrots, sliced*
3 *cups hot, cooked rice*

Have butcher tenderize steak or pound until thin. Cut into 1-inch strips. Blend cornstarch, salt, pepper and garlic powder together. Dredge meat in cornstarch mixture. Brown in oil. Add onion. Cook 2 to 3 minutes. Stir in beer, broth, hot pepper sauce and brown sugar. Bring to a boil. Reduce heat. Cover and simmer for 15 minutes. Add carrots. Cook 15 minutes longer or until meat is tender. Spoon over rice.
Serves 4 to 5.

Ethel Lange

Oriental Beef with Pea Pods

2 lbs. *of flank steak, sliced into ¼-inch thick pieces*
2 Tbs. *dry white wine*
2 Tbs. *soy sauce*
1 Tbs. *cornstarch*
2 Tbs. *cooking oil*
⅛ tsp. *ground ginger*
2 *6-oz. pkgs. frozen pea pods*
6-oz. *fresh mushrooms, sliced*
1 *8-oz. can water chestnuts, sliced*
cooked rice

Mix wine, soy sauce and cornstarch together. Pour over meat. Marinate 1 hour at room temperature. Place oil and ginger in a woc or fry pan. Heat to 375°. Meanwhile drain and save the marinade. Put a quarter of the meat in wok. Stir fry for 3 minutes. Push up sides of wok. Repeat in batches until all meat is cooked. Add pea pods. Stir fry 3 minutes. Add mushrooms. Stir fry for 3 minutes. Add water chestnuts. Stir fry for 1 minute. Pour marinade over all. Stir gently. Reduce heat and simmer, covered, for 4 to 5 minutes. Serve with or on cooked rice. Meat can be marinated in the morning. Cover and chill. Have other ingredients prepared before heating wok. Serves 6 to 8.

Ann Horwitz

Entrees: Meat

German Beef Stew

An unusual but tasty combination of vegetables and apple.

1½ lbs. stewing beef, cut into
  1-inch cubes
2 Tbs. cooking oil
1 cup shredded carrots
1 large apple, cored and diced
1 medium onion, sliced
1 cup water
⅓ cup dry red wine
2 beef bouillon cubes
1 clove garlic, minced
½ tsp. anchovy paste
⅛ tsp. thyme, crushed
1 bay leaf
1 Tbs. cornstarch
¼ cup cold water
4 cups hot, cooked noodles
¼ tsp. poppy seed

In large saucepan or Dutch oven, brown meat, half at a time, in hot oil. Add carrots, apple, onion, 1 cup water, wine, bouillon cubes, garlic, paste, thyme and bay leaf. Cover and cook over low heat for 1½ hours or until beef is tender. Remove bay leaf. Combine cornstarch and ¼ cup water. Add to beef mixture. Cook and stir till thickened and bubbly. Arrange hot noodles on large serving platter. Sprinkle with poppy seed. Spoon stew over noodles. Serves 6.

Priscilla Heinecke

Wine-Sauced Round Steak

1½ lbs. round steak, cut into
  serving pieces
2 Tbs. flour
¼ tsp. salt
dash of pepper
2 Tbs. vegetable oil
½ cup dry red wine
¼ cup water
1 3-oz. can sliced mushrooms
¼ cup chopped onion
1 Tbs. chopped parsley
¼ tsp. salt
¼ tsp. basil, crushed
1 Tbs. cornstarch
¼ cup water

Dredge meat with flour, salt and pepper mixture. Brown in hot oil. Add wine, water, mushrooms, onion, parsley, salt and basil to meat. Simmer, covered, for 1¼ hours. Remove meat. Measure pan juices and add water to make ¾ cup liquid. Return liquid to pan. Blend. Blend cornstarch and water together. Add to pan juice. Cook, stirring constantly, until mixture thickens and bubbles. Pass sauce with meat. Serves 4 to 5.

Sharon Roderick

Entrees: Meat

Sauerbraten

3 to 6 lb. boneless rump roast
1 tsp. salt
½ tsp. pepper
4 bay leaves
½ tsp. peppercorns
8 whole cloves
2 medium onions, sliced
1 small carrot, thinly sliced
1 stalk of celery, chopped
1½ cups red wine vinegar
2½ cups water
¼ cup butter

gravy:
2 Tbs. sugar
½ cup water
6 gingersnaps, crushed

Thoroughly rub meat with salt and pepper. Place in a deep earthenware crock or ovenware glass bowl. Add the spices and vegetables. Heat the vinegar and water to boiling. Pour hot over the meat. Let cool. Cover bowl tightly. Refrigerate. Let marinate 48 to 72 hours, turning the meat twice a day.

When ready to cook, remove meat from marinade. Dry with paper towels. Melt butter in a Dutch oven or kettle. Brown meat well on all sides. Strain the marinade and pour over the meat. Cover tightly. Simmer slowly for 2½ to 3 hours or until fork tender. Remove meat to a warmed serving platter. Slice and keep warm while making gravy.

To make 2 cups gravy, melt sugar in a skillet, stirring constantly until golden brown. Gradually stir in 1½ cups hot marinade and water. Add gingersnap crumbs, stirring well until they dissolve and thicken mixture. Serve with potato dumplings. Serves 8 to 10.

Marian Miller

Beef Arlesienne

2 lbs. boneless pot roast
2 Tbs. oil
½ cup dry red wine
2 cups canned tomatoes
¾ cup sliced mushrooms
½ cup consomme
1 clove garlic, crushed
salt and pepper
1 bay leaf
12 pitted black olives

Heat oil in a heavy skillet. Add meat, cooking until well-browned on all sides. Add wine. Cook for 3 minutes longer. Add remaining ingredients. Bring to a boil. Cover tightly. Simmer for 3 to 4 hours, turning meat occasionally and adding more consomme if needed. Serves 4 to 6.

Julie Revane

Entrees: Meat

Lazy Jane's Beef Casserole

Adding potatoes and carrots would make a complete meal.

1 lb. beef chuck or sirloin tip, cut into 2-inch cubes
1 medium onion, sliced and separated into rings
½ cup burgundy
1 10-oz. can consomme, undiluted
¼ cup fine dry bread crumbs
¼ cup sifted flour
¾ tsp. salt
⅛ tsp. pepper

Put uncooked meat into a casserole. Add onion rings. Combine burgundy and consomme in a small bowl. Mix together the crumbs, flour, salt and pepper. Stir into the burgundy mixture. Pour over the meat. Bake at 300° for 3 hours. Do not cover to allow mixture to thicken. Check after 2 hours. Serves 3 to 4.

Carol Tishler

Pepper Steak

1½ lbs. round steak
paprika
2 Tbs. butter
1 clove garlic, minced
1⅓ cups water
1 10½-oz. can beef consomme
4 small onions, cut in wedges
2 medium green peppers, cut in 1-inch strips
⅓ cup soy sauce
3 Tbs. cornstarch
½ lb. fresh mushrooms, sliced
3 medium tomatoes, cut into thin wedges
hot cooked rice

Trim fat from steak. Cut into 1-inch strips. Sprinkle with paprika. Let stand 15 minutes. Melt butter in a large skillet. Add garlic. Add meat and brown. Add 1 cup of the water. Cover. Simmer until meat is tender, about 1 hour. Stir in consomme, onions and green peppers. Cook over low heat for 15 minutes. In a small bowl, mix together the soy sauce, ⅓ cup water and cornstarch. Add to meat mixture. Cook, stirring gently, until thickened. Stir in mushrooms. Cook 10 minutes longer. About 5 minutes before serving, add tomatoes. Serve over rice. Serves 6.

Marion Wolfe

Entrees: Meat

Brisket of Beef a la Bercy

An inexpensive yet tasty dish to serve company.

5 lbs. brisket of beef
marinade:
  2 tsp. seasoned salt
  1 tsp. salt
  1 cup ketchup
  3 Tbs. brown sugar
  1½ cups white vinegar
  2 medium onions, sliced
  1 cup celery leaves, chopped

Mix together the marinade ingredients. Pour over meat which has been placed in a foil-lined pan. Cover. Let stand overnight in refrigerator. When ready to cook, spread onions and celery leaves on top of meat. Bake, uncovered, at 300° for 2 hours. Cover. Bake 3 hours more, basting occasionally. Remove meat from pan. Let stand until cold and firm. Slice very thin on a diagonal. Return to pan. Reheat in gravy.
Serves 18 to 20.

Lolita Truss

Beer Stew

2 lbs. chuck roast, cubed
2 Tbs. butter
2 Tbs. oil
2 Tbs. brandy
2 large onions, sliced
2 Tbs. flour
salt and pepper to taste
1 cup beer
½ cup beef broth
1 bay leaf
¼ tsp. allspice
2 Tbs. sour cream

Brown beef in butter and oil. Add rest of ingredients, except sour cream. Simmer for 2 to 3 hours, or until tender. If you wish, thicken gravy with cornstarch mixed with water. Before serving stir in sour cream. Serve over noodles. Serves 6.

Ann Horwitz

•

A la mode, the French for "in the fashion of" has a completely different meaning for Americans and the French. Whereas in French cooking it describes a beef pot roast braised with vegetables and simmered in a sauce, we use the term as cake, pie or any dessert served with ice cream.

•

Entrees: Meat

No Peek Beef Stew

An easy to make meal for the busy cook, with a good flavor and good consistency.

2 lbs. beef stew meat
1 cup sliced celery
1 cup sliced onions
3 Tbs. tapioca
2 tsp. salt
5 or 6 carrots, cut into pieces
3 potatoes, pared and quartered
1 tsp. brown sugar
2 cups tomato juice
2 bay leaves, optional
½ tsp. thyme, optional
1 tsp. oregano, optional

In a 9x13-inch baking pan, place meat, vegetables, salt, sugar and tapioca. Mix well. Pour tomato juice over all. Cover tightly with foil. Bake at 250° for 4¼ to 5 hours. Serves 6 to 8.

Julie Revane

Stifado (Greek Beef Stew)

4 lbs. beef chuck roast, cut into 1-inch cubes
⅔ cup oil
1 6-oz. can tomato paste
1½ cups dry red wine
8 whole peppercorns
2 bay leaves
½ to 1 Tbs. allspice, to taste
2 garlic cloves, halved
5 whole cloves
salt and pepper to taste
3 lbs. small white onions

Saute meat in oil. Add all but the onions. Bring to a boil. Simmer, covered, for 1 hour, or until tender. Add more wine as needed. Add onions. Cook another 30 to 40 minutes. Canned onions can be used. If so, reduce cooking time to about 20 minutes. Remove bay leaves, garlic and cloves. Sauce will be thick. Serve over noodles to which butter and poppy seeds have been added, if you wish. Serves 8.

Ann Horwitz

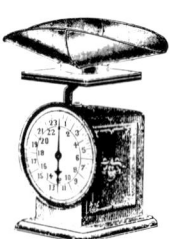

Entrees: Meat

Meat Balls with Caper Sauce

2 slices bread, torn into bits
½ cup skim milk
½ lb. ground beef
¼ lb. ground veal
¼ lb. ground pork
1 medium onion, minced
4 anchovy fillets, chopped, or
   1½ tsp. anchovy paste
2 egg whites
salt and pepper to taste
3 cups water
1 bay leaf
1 small onion, halved
2 peppercorns

sauce:
2 Tbs. butter or margarine
2 Tbs. flour
2 cups strained meat juice
2 Tbs. capers, rinsed and drained
1 Tbs. lemon juice
½ tsp. Dijon mustard
salt and pepper to taste

Soak bread in milk. In a bowl mix moistened bread with meats, onion, anchovy, egg whites, salt and pepper. Mix well. Form into balls about 1½-inches in diameter. In a large frying pan, heat water with a bay leaf, onion and peppercorns. Add meat balls. Simmer gently, covered, for about 20 minutes or until meat is cooked. Remove meat balls from pan. Strain and reserve juice. To make sauce, melt butter. Add flour and stir to form a paste. Slowly add rest of ingredients. Simmer, stirring, until slightly thickened. Return meat balls to pan and heat well before serving.
Serves 4 to 6.

Elizabeth Pleier

Entrees: Meat

Norwegian Meatballs

Serve with boiled potatoes and a can of red cabbage mixed with a can of apple sauce, heated, for a typical Norwegian meal.

1½ cups soft bread crumbs
½ cup milk
1 lb. lean ground beef
½ lb. lean ground pork
¼ cup minced onion
¼ tsp. allspice
½ tsp. nutmeg
1 to 1½ tsp. salt
⅛ tsp. pepper
1 egg, slightly beaten
2 Tbs. vegetable oil
3 Tbs. flour
1 10½-oz. can condensed
    consomme

Mix bread crumbs and milk together in a small bowl. Let stand. In a large bowl combine beef, pork, onion, spices and egg. Mix well. Add moistened bread crumbs. Mix well. Shape mixture into approximately 36 small balls, an inch or so in diameter. Brown over medium heat in hot oil until thoroughly cooked. Remove balls from pan. Blend flour into pan drippings, cooking until lightly brown. Stir in consomme, cooking until gravy thickens. Meat balls can be frozen. Serves 7 to 9.

Peg Nelson

Meat Loaf with Piquant Sauce

A good basic recipe with a tangy sauce.

⅔ cup dry bread crumbs
1 cup milk
1½ lbs. ground beef
2 eggs, slightly beaten
¼ cup grated onion
1 tsp. salt
⅛ tsp. pepper
½ tsp. sage
sauce:
    3 Tbs. brown sugar
    ¼ cup ketchup
    ¼ tsp. nutmeg
    1 tsp. dry mustard

Soak bread crumbs in milk. Add meat, eggs, onion and seasonings. Mix well. Form into a loaf. Place in a greased loaf pan. Combine sauce ingredients. Spread over top of loaf. Bake at 350° about 1 hour.
Serves 6.

Beverly Jaeger

•

Jambalaya, a creole dish, is derived from the French word for ham, "jambon", one of the ingredients. But seafood or any leftover meats also can be used as an ingredient.

•

Entrees: Meat

Party Sweet-Sour Pork

1½ lbs. lean shoulder pork, cut into
    2x½-inch strips
2 Tbs. fat
½ cup water
2 Tbs. cornstarch
½ tsp. salt
¼ cup brown sugar
⅓ cup vinegar
1 cup pineapple juice
1 Tbs. soy sauce
2 tomatoes, cut in wedges
1 onion, thinly sliced
1 20-oz. can pineapple chunks
green pepper strips, optional

Brown pork in hot fat. Add ½ cup water. Cover. Simmer 1 hour. Combine the cornstarch, salt, brown sugar, vinegar, juice and soy sauce in a saucepan. Cook over medium heat until slightly thickened and clear, stirring constantly. Pour sauce over hot pork. Let stand at least 10 minutes. Add remaining ingredients. Cook 2 or 3 minutes. Serve with hot rice or pour into the center of a rice ring. Serves 4 to 6.

Julie Revane

Mandarin Porc a la Creme

1 tsp. grated orange rind
1 tsp. grated lemon rind
¼ tsp. sage
¼ tsp. pepper
1 tsp. salt
4 pork chops or thick pork
    tenderloin patties
1 Tbs. butter
1 Tbs. minced parsley
1 Tbs. Worcestershire sauce
1 cup orange juice
1 can mandarin oranges, drained
sour cream
orange marmalade
cooked rice

Mix orange and lemon rinds, sage, salt and pepper together. Coat chops with mixture. Brown on both sides in the butter. Sprinkle with parsley. Add Worcestershire sauce and orange juice. Cover. Simmer 45 to 60 minutes depending on thicknesss of chops (30 minutes for patties). If necessary, thicken pan juices with cornstarch. Add oranges. Heat through. Arrange on bed of cooked rice. Top with pan juices. Dab each chop with sour cream and marmalade. Garnish with additional oranges. Serves 4.

Betty Peterson

Entrees: Meat

Hawaiian Glazed Spareribs

3 lbs. meaty spareribs
1 onion, quartered
salt to taste
glaze:
  1 6-oz. can frozen pineapple-
    orange juice
  1 tsp. cornstarch
  ⅓ cup barbeque sauce
  ⅓ cup firmly packed brown sugar
  1 Tbs. corn oil
  1 tsp. salt
  1 tsp. dried onion flakes

Place ribs in a large kettle. Add onions, salt and water to cover. Simmer for 1 to 1½ hours. To make the glaze, blend the juice with the cornstarch in a saucepan. Add remaining ingredients. Bring to a boil, stirring constantly. Simmer for 10 minutes. When ribs are cooked, line a roasting pan with the ribs, pour on half of the glaze and add just enough water to pan to cover bottom. Keep adding water during cooking to prevent glaze from burning. Bake at 350° for 1 hour. Turn ribs over, add remaining glaze and reduce temperature to 300°. Bake at least 30 minutes longer. Baste ribs occasionally during entire cooking time, checking each time for the addition of water. Do not add water the last 15 minutes of cooking time so glaze thickens. Serves 4.

Barbara Luetzow

Elegant Spareribs

2 sides, 2 lbs. each, of spareribs
salt and pepper
monosodium glutamate
clove garlic, minced
¼ cup brown sugar
¼ cup soy sauce
1 Tbs. peeled, minced fresh ginger
  root or ½ tsp. ground ginger
1 large onion
1 large green pepper
2 Tbs. cooking oil
1 Tbs. cornstarch
2 Tbs. cider vinegar
1 1 lb. 4-oz. can pineapple chunks,
  drained, reserving 1 cup syrup

Sprinkle ribs lightly with salt, pepper and monosodium glutamate. Place in a shallow pan. Roast uncovered at 425° for 30 minutes. Meanwhile, prepare sauce. Mix together the garlic, soy sauce, brown sugar and ginger. Peel onion. Cut into eighths. Then cut each piece in half. Separate into layers. Cut a seeded green pepper into similar large pieces. Heat oil. Toss in vegetables. Cook, stirring, until shiny, about 1 minute. Add to soy mixture. Mix cornstarch with vinegar and drained syrup. Add to vegetable mixture. Cook for 5 to 10 minutes, stirring frequently. Toss in pineapple. Drain fat from ribs. Pour sauce over. Reduce oven heat to 350°. Bake uncovered 45 minutes to 1 hour longer, or until tender. Ribs should be turned and basted occasionally. Serves 4 to 6.

Gloria Schranz

Entrees: Meat

Barbequed Spareribs

4 lbs. lean pork ribs
1 medium onion, chopped
2 Tbs. butter or margarine
2 Tbs. cider vinegar
4 Tbs. lemon juice
2 Tbs. brown sugar
dash cayenne pepper
1 cup ketchup
2 Tbs. Worcestershire sauce
½ tsp. dry mustard
dash celery salt

Brown ribs in a hot oven. Pour off fat. In a saucepan saute onions in butter until soft. Add remaining ingredients. Simmer briefly to blend flavors. Pour sauce over ribs. Bake at 300° for 2 hours or until tender. Sauce may be made ahead of time and refrigerated. Serves 4 to 6.

Elizabeth Pleier

Oven Fried Pork Chops

4 large, lean pork chops
1 egg, slightly beaten
3 Tbs. soy sauce
1 Tbs. water
⅛ tsp. ground ginger er
½ tsp. garlic powder
4 Tbs. dry bread crumbs

Mix together soy sauce, water and seasonings. Dip chops in soy sauce mixture. Dust with bread crumbs. Place on a cookie sheet. Bake at 350° for 30 minutes. Turn. Bake another 15 minutes, longer if chops are quite thick. Do not overbake. Serves 4.

Ann Horwitz

Spanish Pork Chops

4 pork chops, cut ¾-inch thick
1 Tbs. fat
½ cup regular rice, uncooked
1 cup sliced onions
¼ cup chopped green pepper
1½ tsp. salt
⅛ tsp. pepper
1 tsp. sugar
1 lb. 12-oz. can tomatoes, cut in small pieces

Melt fat in frying pan. Brown chops on both sides. Move chops to side of pan, adding rice to center. Sprinkle remaining ingredients over chops and rice. Heat to boiling. Cover. Reduce heat. Cook about 1 hour, or until meat is tender. Serves 4.

Marian Miller

Entrees: Meat

Baked Ham Loaf

The sauce adds spice and is a change-of-pace from the normal sweet-sour type.

¾ lb. smoked ham, ground fine
½ lb. lean pork, ground fine
½ lb. beef rump or chuck, ground fine
¼ to½ tsp. salt
3 Tbs. chopped onion
¾ cup fine dry bread crumbs
1 egg, beaten
¾ cup milk
apple-horseradish sauce:
　2 large, green apples
　⅛ tsp. cinnamon
　⅛ tsp. white pepper
　¼ cup grated horseradish
　3 Tbs. sugar
　2 tsp. lemon juice

Combine all the loaf ingredients together. Knead until spongy. Shape into a loaf or press into a bread pan. Bake at 350° in an oven which has not been preheated, for 1½ hours. To make sauce, peel, core and steam apples until tender. Mash to a smooth sauce. Add remaining ingredients. Simmer about 5 minutes. Cool. Makes about 1 cup of sauce. Serve ham loaf, hot or cold, with sauce. Serves 6 to 8.

Pearl Hunkel

Glazed Ham Loaves
with Horseradish Sauce

2 lbs. ground ham
1 lb. ground pork
1 8-oz. can tomato sauce
2 eggs
1 onion, chopped
1 cup cracker crumbs
1 cup milk
glaze:
　¾ cup brown sugar
　¼ cup water
　¼ cup vinegar
　2 tsp. dry mustard
horseradish sauce:
　½ cup heavy cream, whipped
　¼ cup creamed horseradish
　1 Tbs. Dijon mustard
　1½ Tbs. vinegar
　¼ to ½ tsp. salt
　4 drops Worcestershire sauce
　dash of cayenne pepper
　dash of paprika

Combine meats, tomato sauce, eggs, onion, crumbs and milk. Mix well. Form into 12 individual loaves. Place in a heavy baking pan. Bake at 350° for 1 hour, basting with the glaze the last ½ hour. To make the glaze, combine all ingredients in a saucepan. Heat until sugar is dissolved. Pass the horseradish sauce with the ham balls. To make the sauce, carefully blend together all the ingredients. Serves 12.

Barbara Luetzow

Entrees: Meat

Ragout of Lamb

5 lbs. of lamb, cubed, with some
  bones
1 large Spanish onion, chopped
2 Tbs. cooking oil
¼ cup flour
salt and pepper
1 cup light, red wine
2 large tomatoes, peeled, seeded
  and chopped
stock (a mixture of beef and chicken
  broth), enough to cover meat
bouquet garni:
  white part of 1 leek
  1 celery stalk with leaves
  1 carrot halved plus 2 tops
  2 lemon peels
  1 bay leaf
  2 sprigs parsley
  ¼ tsp. thyme
1 can water chestnuts, sliced

In heavy casserole, saute onion in oil
until soft not browned. Set aside.
Dredge meat in flour, salt and
pepper. Brown meat, a few pieces at
a time, in a skillet. As meat browns,
add to casserole. Deglaze skillet with
wine, scraping up brown bits. Add to
casserole. Add tomatoes and stock.
Add bouquet garni, which has been
placed in a double thickness of
cheese cloth and tied. Heat to
simmering on top of stove. Then
place in a preheated 250° oven.

Bake for 1½ hours or until tender.
Remove bones and bouquet garni.
Strain juices if you wish. Return to
casserole. Add water chestnuts and
cook another 10 minutes. If sauce is
too thin, thicken with 2 tablespoons
cornstarch in 4 tablespoons water.
May be prepared in advance and
reheated. Serves 6 to 8.

Elizabeth Pleier

Veal Tangelo

2 lbs. veal shoulder or rump
1 tangelo, peeled
1 cup white wine
1 tsp. garlic powder
1 tsp. salt
½ tsp. pepper
¼ cup cornstarch

Squeeze juice over veal. Break pulp
into pieces. Place on meat. Combine
wine, garlic, salt and pepper. Pour
over veal. Bake, covered, at 350°
for approximately 2 hours. Uncover
the last ½ hour of cooking time.
When veal is tender, strain gravy,
adding cornstarch to thicken. Serves
4 to 6.

Lydia Kniephoff

Entrees: Poultry

Chicken Breasts Mediterranean

A robust flavored dish in the Italian manner.

6 *large whole chicken breasts, skinned, boned, halved and flattened slightly*
1 *Tbs. olive oil*
1 *Tbs. unsalted butter*
1 *large onion, chopped*
1 *16-oz. can whole plum tomatoes, drained and chopped*
½ *cup dry marsala wine*
2 *cloves garlic, chopped*
½ *tsp. dried basil*
½ *tsp. oregano*
¼ *tsp. thyme*
¼ *tsp. crumbled bay leaf*
½ *tsp. coriander*
¼ *tsp. fennel seed*
fresh ground pepper
1 *piece orange peel*
minced parsley
parmesan cheese

Saute chicken in butter and oil until cooked through, about 3 minutes per side, or bake at 350° for 30 minutes. Make sauce at least 8 hours in advance to blend flavors.
To make sauce: Cook onion until golden. Add all ingredients except parsley. Simmer for 1 hour. Puree in food processor until still somewhat lumpy. Add parsley and cool. Divide and spread sauce evenly over breasts. Sprinkle with parmesan cheese. Broil until bubbly. Serves 8 to 10.

Elizabeth Pleier

Easy Chicken Dish

4 *chicken breast halves*
1 *10-oz. can cream of mushroom soup*
½ *cup sherry wine*

Put chicken breasts, skin side up, in an 8x8-inch baking dish. Combine soup and wine. Pour over chicken. Bake at 325° for 1 hour. Serves 4.

Marie Grayer

•

The Bay leaf, which gives such a wonderful flavor to vegetables, soups and stews, comes from the laurel shrub or small tree native to the Mediterranean and Near East. In Greece the tree grows to heights over 50 feet and has been a part of their life and mythology. Placing a laurel leaf on the forehead of an Olympic winner led to the phrase "winning one's laurels." Gods, emperors and heroes of ancient Rome also were crowned with laurel.

•

98

Chicken Korean

12 *chicken drumsticks*
½ *cup olive oil*
½ *cup soy sauce*
½ *cup dry white wine*
½ *cup sliced green onions*
2 *cloves garlic, minced*
½ *tsp. freshly ground black pepper*
½ *tsp. dry mustard*
2 *tsp. ground ginger*

Combine all ingredients except chicken. Mix well. Add chicken legs. Marinate in refrigerator for 24 hours. Remove chicken from marinade. Place in a buttered baking dish. Pour a small amount of marinade over top. Cover tightly. Bake at 350° for 1 hour, removing cover the last 15 minutes of cooking time to brown. Serves 6.

Virginia Feind

Cornish Hens a l'Orange

Sauce also can be used on chicken.

4 *Cornish game hens, split in half*
4 *Tbs. butter*
1 *6-oz. can frozen orange juice concentrate*
¾ *cup water*
2 *Tbs. steak sauce*
2 *Tbs. honey*
1 *tsp. salt*
1 *tsp. rosemary, crushed*

Brown split hens in butter in a large skillet. Remove and keep warm. Stir remaining ingredients into skillet, scraping to loosen brown bits. Heat to bubbling. Return hens to skillet, reduce heat, cover and simmer, basting sveral times, for 1¼ hours or until tender when pierced with a fork. Can be prepared in morning and reheated. Serves 6 to 8.

Bobbe Blumberg

Chicken Breasts Perigourdine

6 small whole chicken breasts,
   boned
½ cup corn oil, divided
4 whole scallions, thinly sliced
¼ lb. fresh mushrooms, chopped
½ lb. chicken livers
2 cups soft bread cubes
½ tsp. herbs (rosemary, thyme or
   savory)
½ cup shredded Swiss cheese
½ tsp. salt
¾ cup chicken broth
1 Tbs. flour
½ cup half and half cream
¼ tsp. salt
lemon slices, halved
chopped parsley

Place chicken breasts between wax paper. Flatten with a heavy skillet. Heat ¼ cup oil in saucepan. Add scallions, mushrooms and livers. Cook until livers are slightly browned. Remove livers. Chop and return to pan. Combine the bread cubes, herbs, cheese and ½ teaspoon salt. Add to cooked liver mixture for the dressing. Place breasts skin side down on a flat surface. Sprinkle with ¼ teaspoon salt. Place about ⅓ cup dressing on center of each breast. Fold sides over and fasten with a toothpick. Heat remaining ¼ cup oil in a skillet. Brown breasts on all sides, turning carefully. When brown add ¼ cup of the broth. Cover. Simmer 30 minutes. Remove from skillet and keep warm. Add flour to pan drippings, blending well. Add remaining broth, cream and salt. Cook, stirring constantly, until thickened. Spoon over breasts. Garnish with ½ lemon slices and parsley. Serves 6.

Lolita Truss

Entrees: Poultry

Chicken Breasts with Yogurt Sauce

Serve with artichoke hearts and rice pilaf for an elegant, flavorful meal.

4 chicken breasts, skinned, boned and halved
4 Tbs. butter or margarine
2 Tbs. flour
1/2 cup chicken broth
1/4 cup dry white wine
3/4 cup plain yogurt
2 tsp. grated lemon peel
1/4 cup sliced green onions
1/2 to 1 cup sliced fresh mushrooms

Melt 2 tablespoons butter in baking pan. Add chicken. Bake at 350° for 30 minutes, turning breasts occasionally to coat with butter. Make a sauce of remaining butter, flour, broth, wine, yogurt and lemon peel. Add onions and mushrooms to chicken. Cover with sauce and bake another 30 minutes. Serves 4.

Elizabeth Pleier

Easy Baked Chicken and Rice in Sherry

2 frying chickens, cut in pieces
2/3 cup dry sherry
1 1/2 cups uncooked rice
1 pkg. dry onion soup
2 10 1/2-oz. cans of any combination of creamed soups
1/4 to 1/2 cup water

Mix sherry with rice in a large baking dish. Lay chicken pieces on top. Sprinkle with dry onion soup. Add creamed soups and water. Cover with foil and seal tightly. Bake at 300° for 2 1/4 hours. Serves 8.

Julie Revane

Entrees: Poultry

Chicken Roll Ups

3 large chicken breasts, skinned, boned and halved
6 thin slices boiled ham
3 slices mozzarella cheese, halved
1 medium tomato, chopped
½ tsp. sage, crushed
⅓ cup fine dried bread crumbs
2 Tbs. grated parmesan cheese
2 Tbs. snipped fresh parsley
4-6 Tbs. butter, melted

Cover chicken, boned side up with clear plastic. Working from center out, pound meat lightly to a 5x5-inch piece. Remove plastic. Place ham slice and cheese slice on each cutlet, cutting to fit. Top with some tomato and dash of sage. Tuck in sides. Roll up jelly roll style, pressing to seal well. Combine crumbs, cheese and parsley. Dip chicken in butter, then roll in crumb mixture. Place rolls in a shallow baking pan. Bake at 350° for 40 to 45 minutes. Serves 6.

Mildred Booth

Chicken Ratatouille

2 whole chicken breasts, skinned, boned and cut into 1-inch pieces
¼ cup cooking oil
2 small zucchini, unpared, thinly sliced
1 small eggplant, peeled, cut into 1-inch cubes
1 large onion, thinly sliced
1 medium green pepper, seeded, cut into 1-inch pieces
½ lb. mushrooms, sliced
1 16-oz. can tomato wedges or 3 fresh tomatoes cut into small wedges
2 tsp. garlic salt
1 tsp. sweet basil, crushed
1 tsp. dried parsley
½ tsp. fresh ground pepper
hot cooked rice

Heat oil in large skillet. Add chicken. Saute about 2 minutes on each side. Add zucchini, eggplant, onion, green pepper and mushrooms. Cook over medium heat, stirring occasionally, about 15 minutes or until tender-crisp. Add tomatoes, stirring gently. Add seasonings. Simmer about 5 minutes or until chicken is fork tender. Serve on a large platter with a mound of rice in the center. Serves 4.

Priscilla Heinecke

Entrees: Poultry

DeLuxe Party Chicken Breasts

An easy recipe if butcher does the deboning.

1   4-oz. pkg. chipped, dried beef,
    finely chopped
6   whole chicken breasts, skinned,
    boned and halved
6   slices bacon
1   8-oz. carton sour cream
2   10½-oz. cans cream of mush-
    room soup
2   Tbs. dry vermouth
    grated parmesan cheese
    paprika

Place dried beef in bottom of a 9x12-inch baking dish. Wrap each chicken breast with half a slice of bacon and place on beef. Mix together the sour cream, soup and vermouth. Pour over chicken. Sprinkle on cheese and paprika. Bake at 300° for 2½ hours. Can be prepared the day before, then baked. Serves 6 to 8.

Bobbe Blumberg
Beverly Quirk

Chicken Granada

2½ to 3lbs. chicken pieces
2   tsp. paprika
2   tsp. garlic salt
2   tsp. celery salt
1   cup uncooked rice
1½ cups hot chicken broth
2   tsp. lemon juice
½   tsp. hot pepper sauce
2   Tbs. chopped parsley
⅓   cup sliced pimiento stuffed
    olives

Season chicken with paprika and salts. Bake in a shallow casserole at 425° for 20 minutes. Remove chicken. In same casserole add rice, broth, juice and pepper sauce. Stir well. Arrange chicken pieces on rice. Cover and bake an additional 30 minutes or until chicken is tender and liquid is absorbed. Garnish with olive slices. Serves 6.

Beverly Jaeger

•

Spanish settlers in America liked rice as part of their meals, using it with fresh herbs. Unlike current Spanish rice recipes, very few chilies were used.

•

Entrees: Poultry

Spicy Chicken Hunan

2 whole chicken breasts, boned, cut
   into strips
1 Tbs. sherry
1 Tbs. light soy sauce
1 Tbs. cornstarch
¼ cup peanut oil
1 8-oz. can bamboo shoots,
   drained and diced
2 Tbs. hoisin sauce
¼ tsp. crushed red, hot pepper
1 Tbs. chopped scallion
1 tsp. chopped ginger

Combine sherry, soy sauce and cornstarch, mixing to dissolve cornstarch. Marinate chicken strips in mixture for about 10 minutes, tossing to coat all pieces. Heat oil in a wok. Stir fry chicken for 2 minutes. Remove from wok. Add remaining ingredients. Stir fry for 2 minutes. Return chicken to wok. Mix well. Cover. Cook for 5 minutes or until chicken is tender. Serves 3 to 4.

Audrienne Eder

Waikiki Chicken

Dish can be made ahead and reheated. It also is excellent as a second day leftover.

frying chicken for 4 people
½ cup flour
⅓ cup oil or shortening
1 tsp. salt
¼ tsp. pepper
sauce:
1 can sliced pineapple
1 cup sugar
2 tsp. cornstarch
¾ cup cider vinegar
1 Tbs. soy sauce
¼ to ½ tsp. ground ginger
1 chicken bouillon cube
1 large green pepper, seeded,
   cut crosswise

Wash chicken. Pat dry. Coat with flour. Heat oil in a skillet, add chicken. Brown on all sides. Remove to a shallow roasting pan, arranging pieces skin side up. Sprinkle with salt and pepper. To make sauce, drain pineapple, pouring syrup into 2-cup measure. Add water to make 1¼ cups liquid. In a medium saucepan combine the sugar, cornstarch, vinegar, soy sauce, ginger, bouillon cube and pineapple liquid. Bring to a boil, stirring constantly. Boil for 2 minutes. Pour over chicken. Bake at 350° for 30 minutes, uncovered. Add pineapple slices and green pepper. Bake 30 minutes longer or until chicken is tender. Serve with rice. Serves 4.

Carol Tishler

Pineapple Chicken

A change-of-pace way to serve chicken.

2½ lbs. boned chicken breasts
¼ cup flour
1 tsp. salt
½ tsp. pepper
¼ tsp. thyme
5 Tbs. butter
¼ lb. sharp cheddar cheese, grated
½ lb. cooked ham, cut into strips
1 4-oz. can sliced mushrooms
1 14-oz. can pineapple tidbits

Combine flour, salt, pepper and thyme. Roll chicken in seasoned flour. Brown in the butter, turning to brown all sides. Transfer chicken to a 2-quart casserole. Sprinkle on the cheese and ham. Add mushrooms with liquid. Drain pineapple, reserving ¼ cup syrup. Add pineapple and reserved liquid to casserole. Bake covered at 350° for 40 to 60 minutes. Remove cover and bake 10 minutes longer. Serves 4 to 6.

Lydia Kniephoff

Chicken South Sea

1 3 to 3½ lb. fryer chicken
4 Tbs. cornstarch
6 Tbs. water
½ cup vinegar
½ cup sugar
⅛ cup soy sauce
1 tsp. salt
½ to 1 tsp. pepper
1 Tbs. Worcestershire sauce
1 20-oz. can crushed pineapple or pineapple chunks

Cut up the chicken. Skin can be removed to cut calories. Place in a lightly greased 9x13-inch baking dish. In a medium-sized saucepan, combine cornstarch and water, blending well. Add all but the pineapple. Cook over medium heat until mixture thickens. Add pineapple. Cook until well blended. Pour over chicken. Cover with foil. Bake at 350° for 1¼ hours or until chicken is fork tender. Can be prepared ahead of time and refrigerated, then baked, adding 15 minutes or so to cooking time. Serves 4.

Judy De Vries

Entrees: Poultry

Turkey Schnitzel

This turkey meat can be used for any recipe that calls for veal schnitzel or scallops.

½ *turkey breast, skinned and boned*
salt and pepper
flour
beaten egg
dry bread crumbs
butter
parsley
lemon wedges

Remove the turkey fillet (piece closest to breast bone). Slice the "hump" off the breast meat. This meat can be used for other dishes. Slice the remaining flat breast meat, against the grain, into butterfly pieces. Cut once all the way through, the next ¾ way through, the next all the way through. Flatten piece and pound to about ¼ inch thick. Season slices with salt and pepper. Dust with flour, dip in egg, then in bread crumbs. Saute in butter until golden brown, about 5 minutes. Garnish with parsley and lemon wedges. Yield depends on size of turkey breast.

Elizabeth Pleier

Duck with Plum Sauce

A sharp, pungent sauce that adds flavor and moisture to the duck. Leftover sauce can be frozen and used with cut up chicken.

1   *4 to 5 lb. fresh or frozen duck*
3   *apples, peeled and cored*
1   *medium onion, chopped*
2   *Tbs. butter*
1   *17-oz. can pitted purple plums*
1   *6-oz. can frozen lemonade*
¼   *cup soy sauce*
2   *tsp. prepared mustard*
1   *tsp. ground ginger*
1   *tsp. Worcestershire sauce*
2   *drops hot pepper sauce*

Wash duck, pat dry, and stuff with apples. Prick skin several times with a sharp knife. Saute onion in butter. Puree plums with syrup in a blender or food mill. Add to onions. Add remaining ingredients. Simmer 15 minutes. Place duck on a rack. Roast at 400° for 30 minutes. Reduce heat to 350° and roast for 2 hours or until tender, basting with plum sauce during last 30 minutes of roasting time. Serves 4.

Bobbe Blumberg

Entrees: Seafood

Shrimp Creole I

3 Tbs. butter or margarine
2 medium onions, chopped
1/2 green pepper, chopped
1/2 cup chopped celery
1 clove garlic, minced
1 1/2 Tbs. flour
1 1-lb. 14-oz. can tomatoes
1 tsp. salt
1 tsp. sugar
2 bay leaves
1/2 tsp. thyme, crushed
1/4 tsp. allspice
1 Tbs. Worcestershire sauce
1 to 1 1/2-lbs. fresh or frozen shrimp,
  cleaned and deveined
2 Tbs. chopped parsley
cooked rice

Melt butter in a skillet. Add onion, green pepper, celery and garlic. Cook until tender but not brown. Blend in flour. Add tomatoes, salt, sugar, bay leaves, thyme, allspice and Worcestershire sauce. Simmer 30 minutes. Remove bay leaves, adding shrimp during the last 5 to 10 minutes of cooking time. Do not overcook. Sprinkle with parsley and serve over hot rice. Serves 6.

Virginia Feind

Shrimp Creole II

Serve with a salad and hot, crusty bread.

3 Tbs. oil
1 medium onion, sliced
1 medium green pepper, coarsely
  chopped
2 8-oz. cans tomato sauce
1/2 bay leaf
about 7-oz. raw, cleaned shrimp or
frozen shrimp, thawed
1/2 tsp. salt
1/8 tsp. black pepper
dash of garlic powder
2 1/2 cups cooked rice
cayenne pepper

Place oil in a 2-quart saucepan. Add onion and green pepper. Cook slowly, stirring occasionally, until tender. Add tomato sauce, bay leaf, shrimp, salt, black pepper and garlic powder. Simmer 15 minutes. Add rice. Heat. Add cayenne pepper to taste. Serves 4 to 6.

Patricia Dulski

Entrees: Seafood

Gifts from the Inland Sea

What to do with fillets of coho or chinook salmon, brown or rainbow trout...actually any fish fillet would be happy with this treatment.

1 to 2 lbs. fish fillets (1 large, 2 medium, 4 small)
1 to 1½ cups milk
4 Tbs. softened butter
3 Tbs. lemon juice
½ tsp. salt
¼ tsp. paprika
¼ tsp. pepper
1 Tbs. minced parsley
¼ cup soft bread crumbs or ¼ cup dried

Remove all snips and tags of skin. If any bones protrude, remove. Soak fillets in enough milk to cover for an hour or so, turning once. Drain. Pat dry with a paper towel. Sprinkle lightly with 1 tablespoon lemon juice. Pre-heat oven to 450°. Line a large, flat baking pan with foil and spread on a little butter or vegetable oil. Pre-heat pan for a few minutes. Combine 2 tablespoons lemon juice with butter, seasonings and parsley. Place fillets on heated pan. Spread on the butter mix and pat in the crumbs. Bake for 5 to 10 minutes, depending on the thickness. Do not overcook! When flesh begins to flake with a fork and milky, translucent look disappears, it's time to serve. Serving with accompanying tartar sauce is optional. Serves 3 to 4.

tartar sauce:
1 cup mayonnaise
1 Tbs. minced chives
1 Tbs. capers, chopped if large
2 Tbs. chopped watercress or 1 Tbs. chopped parsley
1 Tbs. minced pickles
dash of garlic salt

Combine ingredients. Refrigerate a few hours to blend flavors.

Gloria Stanford

•

Creole cooking is native to Louisiana and the Gulf states, where original Spanish and French settlers were anxious to maintain their heritage, culture and language. Dishes that are familiar to us are bouillabaisse, gumbos and jambalyas all using seafoods and seasonings which rely heavily on onions, garlic, pepper and green pepper.

•

Entrees: Seafood

Poached Salmon

This dish is also good when served cold and would make an excellent picnic entree.

3 lbs. of fresh salmon, filleted
white wine, enough to cover bottom
of baking dish
juice of ¼ lemon
salt
dill weed and capers (optional but
good)
butter

Grease bottom of a glass baking dish. Cut fillets into serving size portions and place in dish. Pour on wine but don't drown the fish. Sprinkle on lemon juice. Salt lightly. Sprinkle with dill weed and capers. Dot with butter. Cover with aluminum foil. Bake at 375° for about 10 minutes. Serve with your favorite dill sauce. Serves 6.

Lois Le Vine

Sour Cream Dill Sauce
for Cold Poached Salmon

The sauce enhances rather than overpowers the fish's flavor.

2½ cups mayonnaise
1 cup sour cream
3 Tbs. grated parmesan cheese
3 Tbs. chopped fresh dill or 1 Tbs.
dried dill weed
3 Tbs. minced onion
1 Tbs. plus 1 tsp. cider vinegar
1 tsp. freshly ground pepper
2 Tbs. fresh lemon juice
2 tsp. Worcestershire sauce
2 cloves garlic, crushed

Combine ingredients in food processor or blender and mix well. Chill before serving. Yields 4 cups.

Elizabeth Pleier

Entrees: Seafood

Red Snapper with Almond Sauce

Almond sauce goes well with other fish or seafood or even over baked chicken.

6 thick slices red snapper
flour, seasoned with salt and pepper
1/2 cup butter or margarine
1 medium onion, minced
1 medium green pepper, minced
1 cup blanched, slivered almonds
1/4 cup dry sherry
1 Tbs. lemon juice
pimiento, cut in strips
watercress or parsley

Dust fish lightly with seasoned flour. Melt half the butter in a large skillet. Saute fish until golden brown on both sides. Remove to ovenproof serving platter. Clean skillet with paper toweling. Add remaining butter. Saute onion and green pepper until transparent. Add almonds. Cook until lightly toasted. Stir in wine. Bring to a boil. Pour over fish on platter. Sprinkle with lemon juice. Bake at 400° for 10 to 15 minutes. Remove from oven. Garnish with pimiento and watercress or parsley. Serves 6.

Beverly Jaeger

Baked Whitefish Fillets

2 lbs. whitefish fillets
salt
1/2 cup sour cream
1/2 cup cornflake crumbs
paprika

Cut fillets into serving portions. Line a shallow pan or cookie sheet with foil. Grease well. Lay fish on foil skin side down. Salt fish and spread sour cream over each piece. Sprinkle with crumbs and paprika. Bake at 375° for 35 to 45 minutes, until fish is done but not dry. Serves 4.

Mildred Booth

Fish with Yogurt-Mustard Sauce

1 lb. whitefish
3/4 cup yogurt
1 Tbs. soy sauce
1 Tbs. chopped chives or green onion
1/2 tsp. ground ginger
1 Tbs. Dijon mustard

Pat fish dry and place in an oblong baking dish. Combine remaining ingredients and blend well. Spread over fish. Bake at 425° on top shelf of oven for 10 minutes per inch thickness of fish. Serves 2 to 4.

Judy De Vries

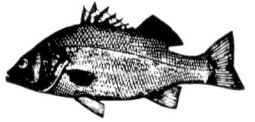

Notes

Vegetables and Accompaniments

Pre-Columbian pottery

Many of the vegetables we use every day were unknown outside the Americas before Columbus. But for hundreds of years throughout Peru, their forms were modeled and painted on ceramics. Corn, beans, squash, peppers and the potato, all molded in clay, are reminders of this ancestry.

Chimu, Nazca, Chavin and Mochica are just some of the many different cultures of ancient Peru where the environment served as an inspiration to early potters. Potatoes and corn, parrots and owls, conch shells and jaguars were parts of this world and appear on their vessels.

Vegetables & Accompaniments

Delicious Vegetable Casserole

1 12-oz. can white shoe-peg corn,
   drained
1 15-oz. can French-cut green
   beans, drained
½ cup chopped celery
½ cup chopped onion
¼ cup chopped green pepper
½ cup sour cream
½ cup grated sharp cheese
salt and pepper to taste

topping:
  ½ box ritz-type crackers,
     crushed fairly fine
¼ cup melted butter or margarine
½ cup blanched, slivered almonds

Combine all but topping ingredients. Mix well. Place in a buttered 9x12-inch baking dish. Mix together the topping ingredients and put on top of vegetable mixture. Bake at 350° for 45 minutes. Serves 6 to 8.

Marie Grayer

Fried Noodles

1 lb. vermicelli
½ tsp. garlic powder
2 Tbs. dark soy sauce
1 Tbs. light soy sauce
1 slice ginger, minced
5 Tbs. peanut oil
2 scallions, sliced

Parboil vermicelli according to package directions. Rinse in cold water. Drain. Mix together the garlic powder, soy sauce and ginger. Place vermicelli in a large, deep skillet. Pour soy sauce mixture over, stirring thoroughly. Heat peanut oil in a small skillet until smoking. Pour over vermicelli. Mix well. Heat until piping hot. Add half of scallions. Mix well. Garnish with remaining scallions. Serves 6 to 8.

Audrienne Eder

•

Early settlers in America were taught how to use root cellars and corn bins by the Indians. The colonists quickly learned to depend on corn as an important staple using it fresh, fried, dried and ground, sometimes as often as three times a day over the harsh winter months. Corn was made into breads, puddings, pies, pancakes and porridges. Even the cobs were used to make jelly.

•

Vegetables & Accompaniments

Stir Fried Mixed Chinese Vegetables

3 Tbs. peanut oil
6 Cloud ears (available in specialty
   food stores and Oriental markets)
1 Tbs. chopped scallions
2 cups bok choy (Chinese greens),
   sliced
2 cups napa
½ cup sliced water chestnuts
½ cup sliced bamboo shoots
½ cup snow pea pods
1 Tbs. water
½ tsp. sugar
pinch of salt

Rinse cloud ears under cold running water. Soak in warm water for 15 minutes. Heat peanut oil in wok. Add cloud ears and scallions. Stir fry a few seconds. Add bok choy and napa. Stir fry 1 minute. Add water chestnuts, bamboo shoots and pea pods. Mix well. Add water. Cover. Cook 1 minute. Add sugar and salt. Stir well. Serve immediately. Serves 4 to 6.

Audrienne Eder

Picnic Potatoes

A buttery rich potato that's easy to prepare.

½ cup butter or margarine
6 to 8 Idaho potatoes
pepper, onion salt, paprika

Melt butter on a cookie sheet. Wash the potatoes well, then slice, unpeeled, into ¼-inch slices. Place on cookie sheet, turning to coat with butter. Sprinkle generously with the seasonings. Bake at 400° for 20 minutes or until tender.
Serves 6 to 8.

Anonymous

116

Vegetables & Accompaniments

Back-for-More Scalloped Potatoes

4 *medium sized potatoes, sliced*
2 *small onions, sliced*
1½ *cups whipping cream*
salt and pepper to taste

Layer potatoes and onions in a lightly-buttered casserole, seasoning to taste, ending with a layer of potatoes. Pour cream over the top. Bake covered at 325° for 1½ hours. Serves 6.

Ann Kratt

Mushrooms Baked in Foil

12 *large mushrooms*
olive or salad oil
seasoned salt
pepper
any other seasonings of your choice

Dip mushrooms in oil. Arrange in one layer on a large piece of heavy foil. Sprinkle with salt, pepper and other seasonings, if desired. Seal. Bake at 350° for 15 to 20 minutes. Serves 2 to 4.

Marie Grayer

Potato Casserole

1 *2-lb. bag frozen hash brown potatoes, thawed*
1 *tsp. salt*
1 *tsp. pepper*
½ *cup chopped onions*
1 *pt. sour cream*
10 *oz. American cheese, grated*
1 *10-oz. can creamed soup*
  (chicken, mushroom or celery)
croutons, crackers or potato chips, crushed
butter, melted

Put all ingredients except crumbs and butter in a large bowl. Mix thoroughly. Put into a greased 13x9-inch baking dish. Sprinkle with crumbs. Drizzle with butter. This may be prepared ahead, covered and refrigerated before baking. Bake at 350° for 50 minutes. May be browned under the broiler if you wish. Serves 10 to 12.

Lolita Truss

Vegetables & Accompaniments

Florentine Tomatoes

A colorful, beautiful-looking side dish to serve with meat, fish or fowl.

6 to 8 tomatoes
1 pkg. spinach souffle, thawed
parmesan cheese
onion salt

Cut tomatoes in half, removing stem. Squeeze gently to remove juice and seeds. Turn upside down. Spoon spinach into tomato halves. Sprinkle with cheese and onion salt. Place in ovenproof dish. Bake at 350° for 30 minutes. Can be prepared in advance and refrigerated.
Serves 6 to 8.

Bobbe Blumberg

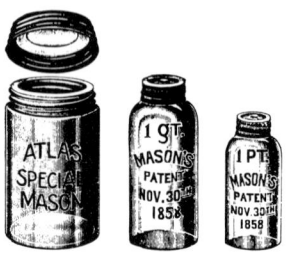

Carrots Lyonnaise

6 medium carrots (about 1 lb.), pared and sliced into julienne strips
1 chicken bouillon cube or 1 tsp. instant chicken bouillon
½ cup boiling water
4 Tbs. butter or margarine
3 medium onions (about 2 cups), sliced
1 Tbs. flour
¼ tsp. salt
dash of pepper
¾ cup water
pinch of sugar

Dissolve bouillon in boiling water. Add carrots. Cook covered for 10 minutes. Meanwhile, melt butter in a skillet. Add onions. Cook, covered, for about 15 minutes, stirring occasionally. Stir in flour, salt and pepper. Add the ¾ cup water and bring to a boil. Add carrots and chicken stock. Simmer, uncovered, about 10 minutes or until carrots are tender. Add sugar just before serving.
Serves 6 to 8.

Peg Nelson

Vegetables & Accompaniments

Oven Carrots

Cook along with an oven meal. Add a can of drained pearl onions for flavor and variety.

18 small carrots, peeled
1/3 cup butter
1/2 to 1 tsp. salt
1/3 to 1/2 cup sugar
1/3 tsp. cinnamon
1/3 cup boiling water

Melt butter. Add salt, sugar and cinnamon, then boiling water and mix. Place carrots in an ovenproof dish and pour mixture over. Cover and bake at 350° for 1½ hours. Serves 6 to 8.

Ann Hill

Bacon-Fried Carrots

3 slices bacon, diced
1 lb. carrots, sliced
1 medium onion, sliced or chopped
1/2 tsp. salt
1/8 tsp. pepper

Cook bacon until crisp. Remove and set aside. Add carrots and onions to bacon fat. Sprinkle with salt and pepper. Cover and cook slowly for 10 minutes or until almost tender. Uncover. Cook, turning until carrots are lightly brown. Add bacon. Serve at once. Serves 4.

Maggie Schimmel

Vegetables & Accompaniments

Celery Root Saute

A "new" vegetable - easy to prepare and delicious.

1 medium celery root
2 Tbs. butter or margarine
1 Tbs. chopped parsley

Remove and discard green top from celery root. Pare and cut into julienne strips. Cook in boiling, salted water until just tender, about 8 minutes. Cook butter until just browned. Pour over celery root. Season to taste. Sprinkle with parsley. Serves 2 to 4.

Peg Nelson

Baked Lima Beans with Garlic Topping

1 lb. dried lima beans
2 carrots, minced
1 medium onion, minced
¼ lb. salt pork, diced
freshly ground pepper
¼ tsp. thyme
1 cup dry white wine or vermouth

topping:
　1 cup dry bread crumbs (home-made preferred)
　½ cup melted butter or combination of butter and oil
　1 to 2 cloves garlic, minced
　½ cup fresh minced parsley

Soak beans overnight. Drain. Cover with cold water. Bring to a boil. Simmer 15 minutes. Drain. Set aside. In a heavy oven-proof casserole, saute salt pork, adding a little oil if necessary to prevent sticking. When pork starts to crisp, add carrots and onions. Cover and wilt. Add lima beans, seasonings and wine. Add enough water to cover. Bring to a boil on top of stove. Then bake at 300° for 1½ to 2 hours or until tender, covering only for half an hour or so. Liquid should cook down. Cover beans with topping. Return to oven for 15 to 30 minutes to brown. Serves 8 to 10.

Elizabeth Pleier

Vegetables & Accompaniments

Spinach Souffle

2   10-oz. pkgs. frozen chopped
    spinach
1   pkg. dry onion soup mix
1   cup sour cream
cracker crumbs, grated parmesan
    cheese, butter

Cook spinach according to package directions, omitting salt. Drain well. Blend onion soup mix into sour cream. Add spinach, mixing well. Pour into a 1½-quart casserole. Top with crumbs, cheese and dot with butter. Bake, covered at 325 to 350° for 30 to 35 minutes. Serves 4 to 6.

Mildred Booth

Special Peas

A different tasting recipe that even non-olive lovers will like.

1   Tbs. butter
2   cups celery, diagonally cut
2   10-oz. pkgs. frozen peas in butter
    sauce
½   cup pitted ripe olives, sliced
½   tsp. dried tarragon, crumbled

Cook celery in butter for 5 minutes. Add peas and cook gently for 10 minutes. Stir in olives and tarragon and heat for 2 minutes. Serves 8.

Sybil La Budde

Vegetables & Accompaniments

Tomato-Corn Casserole

Use in place of potaotes or take to a potluck.

2   16-oz. cans tomatoes, drained
1   8-oz. can tomato sauce
1   12-oz. can whole kernel corn, drained
1   3-oz. can chow mein noodles
1   medium onion, finely chopped
1/2 green pepper, chopped
6   strips bacon, diced

Mix together all ingredients except bacon. Put into a buttered casserole. Top with bacon. Bake at 350° for 40 minutes. Place under broiler a few minutes until bacon is crisp.
Serves 6.

Mary Ceci

Fried Green Tomatoes

A recipe from Mrs. Harry S. Truman that is equally good with pork, pork sausage or lamb chops. A good way to use and not waste unripened tomatoes in the fall. Use green tomatoes that are still a bit firm and do not peel them. Slice tomatoes into 1/4 to 1/2-inch slices, using only the middle slices. Sprinkle with salt, pepper and flour. Fry in butter 4 to 5 minutes per side until lightly browned.

Marie Grayer

Vegetables & Accompaniments

Potato Dumplings

An excellent accompaniment for sauerbraten. Leftovers can be cut into ¼-inch thick slices, browned and served with leftover gravy.

6 medium potatoes (about 2 lbs.), pared
2 eggs, slightly beaten
1 scant cup flour
¾ scant cup farina
⅛ tsp. nutmeg
⅛ tsp. cinnamon
½ tsp. sugar
1 tsp. salt
¼ cup instant minced onion

Boil potatoes and put through a ricer, making about 4½ cups. Let cool. Add remaining ingredients in the order given, mixing well. Roll mixture into balls slightly larger than a golf ball. Place on a cookie sheet. Let stand several hours. To cook, drop into enough boiling salted water to cover, using 1 teaspoon salt to 1 quart of water. Simmer, not boil, for 20 minutes. Lift out with slotted spoon. Serves 8 to 10.

Marian Miller

Southern Corn Custard

3 eggs, well beaten
2 cups canned corn, drained
2 Tbs. butter, melted
2 cups milk
1 tsp. salt
¼ tsp. pepper
½ tsp. sugar
⅓ cup buttered cracker crumbs

Combine eggs, corn, butter and milk. Mix well. Add salt, pepper and sugar. Pour into a buttered 1-quart casserole. Top with crumbs. Bake at 350° for 40 minutes or until custard is firm. Serves 6.

Emma Pagel

Vegetables & Accompaniments

Green Rice

1   cup finely-chopped parsley
2   cups cooked rice
1   lb. American cheese, grated
2   cups milk
2   eggs
¼   cup olive oil
1   medium onion, grated
1   clove garlic, chopped (optional)
salt and pepper to taste

Combine parsley with rice, mixing well. Add milk, cheese, eggs which have been beaten with the olive oil, and remaining ingredients. Mix well. Pour into a buttered 2-quart casserole. Bake at 350° for 1 hour. Serves Serves 8.

Marie Grayer

Puffed-Up Zucchini

A light, tender, souffle-like dish to serve with a roast.

8   cups chopped zucchini
1½ cups chopped onion
½   cup water
4   Tbs. butter or margarine
1   tsp. salt
¼   tsp. pepper
2   eggs, slightly beaten
1½ cups coarse cracker crumbs
4   Tbs. butter or margarine

Combine zucchini and onion in a saucepan. Add water. Cover. Cook until tender, about 15 minutes. Remove from heat. Drain well. Mash zucchini. Add 4 tablespoons butter, salt and pepper. Cool. Add egg and mix thoroughly. Pour into a greased baking dish. Top with crumbs that have been browned in 4 tablespoons of butter. Bake at 350° for 30 minutes. Serves 6.

Pearl Hunkel

Vegetables & Accompaniments

Ginger Sauce for Pears

Serve this side dish the next time you have a Chinese main dish. Also good over rice.

1/3 cup light corn syrup
1/4 cup finely chopped candied
  ginger
dash of salt
1/2 cup light cream
1/4 cup butter
1/2 tsp. vanilla

Combine the corn syrup, ginger, salt and 1/4 cup cream. Simmer 5 minutes. Gradually stir in remaining 1/4 cup cream. Heat through but do not boil. Remove from heat. Stir in butter and vanilla. Serve warm over canned pear halves. Yields 3/4 cup.

Betty Peterson

Scalloped Cabbage

4 cups shredded cabbage
1 10-oz. can cream of potato soup
1/2 cup water
1 cup grated cheddar cheese
bread crumbs

Grate or chop cabbage fine. Put in greased 9x12-inch casserole dish. Pour on soup that has been mixed with water. Sprinkle cheese on top. Bake at 350° until cabbage is done, about 20 minutes. Sprinkle on bread crumbs. Return to oven to brown. Serves 6 to 8.

Marie Grayer

Vegetables & Accompaniments

Spinach Casserole

2 10-oz. pkgs. frozen chopped
    spinach, cooked and well drained
3 hard-cooked eggs, finely chopped
2 Tbs. onion, finely chopped
3 Tbs. butter
3 Tbs. flour
1 tsp. salt
¼ tsp. pepper
⅛ tsp. nutmeg
2 cups milk
½ cup cornflake crumbs
½ cup grated cheddar cheese
2 Tbs. melted butter

Saute onions in butter until transparent. Stir in flour, salt, pepper and
nutmeg. Gradually add the milk,
stirring constantly until sauce is
thickened. Add chopped eggs to
spinach and fold in sauce mixture.
Turn into a 1-quart greased casserole. Combine crumbs, cheese and
butter and spread evenly over spinach. Bake at 375° for 20 to 25
minutes. Serves 6.

Marian Miller

Pecan Pilaf

A good accompaniment for poultry
or beef.

8 Tbs. margarine, divided
1 cup chopped pecans
½ cup chopped onion
2 cups long grain rice
4 cups chicken broth, heated
1 tsp. salt
¼ tsp. thyme
⅛ tsp. pepper
2 Tbs. chopped parsley

Melt 3 tablespoons margarine in a
large skillet or Dutch oven. Add
pecans. Saute 10 minutes, or until
lightly browned. Remove pecans.
Cover and set aside. In same skillet,
melt remaining margarine. Add
onion. Saute until tender. Add rice,
stirring to thoroughly coat the grains.
Add chicken broth, salt, thyme and
pepper. Cover. Simmer 18 to 20
minutes until rice is tender and liquid
is absorbed. Can be made ahead to
this point. Cover and refrigerate up
to 24 hours. To heat, add ¾ cup
water to cooked rice in a skillet.
Cover and heat 5 to 8 minutes, until
hot. Remove from heat. Stir in nuts
and parsley. Serves 8 to 10.

Lynn Falconer

Vegetables & Accompaniments

Scalloped Pineapple

A delicious accompaniment for ham or pork. Different and colorful.

3½ cups canned pineapple chunks, drained, retaining juice
½ lb. sharp cheddar cheese, grated
½ cup flour
½ cup sugar

Grease a 1-quart casserole dish. Arrange a layer of pineapple chunks on bottom. Combine the flour and sugar. Sprinkle on the pineapple. Sprinkle on the cheese. Repeat layers until all ingredients are used. Pour on pineapple juice. Bake at 350° for 45 minutes. Serves 6.

Marie Grayer

•

Both mace and nutmeg come from the nutmeg tree. Mace comes from the netlike membrane that covers the shell around the nutmeg seed. In colonial times, the mace was dried and ground. The nutmeg was kept whole and ground as needed.

•

Italian Eggplant Casserole

Add a pound of cooked ground beef for a complete meal-in-one dish.

1 eggplant
1 onion, coarsely chopped
1 cup bread cubes
1 cup shredded cheddar cheese
1 16-oz. can tomatoes, drained, saving juice
½ tsp. oregano
½ tsp. basil
fresh bread crumbs
butter

Peel and cut eggplant into 1-inch cubes. Boil in salted water with the onion for about 5 minutes. Drain well. In a 2-quart casserole layer eggplant with bread cubes, cheese and tomatoes. Add some tomato juice to moisten. Add oregano and basil. Top with buttered crumbs. Bake at 350° for 30 minutes. Serves 4 to 6.

Julie Revane

Vegetables & Accompaniments

Scalloped Rutabagas and Apples

A tasty accompaniment for roast pork, goose or duck.

1 small rutabaga, pared and
    quartered, sliced ¼-inch thick
2 large apples. quartered and thinly
    sliced
6 Tbs. brown sugar
2 Tbs. butter

Drop rutabaga pieces into boiling, salted water and cook until just tender, about 3 minutes. Drain well. In a 1-quart casserole, arrange slices of apple and rutabaga in an orderly pattern until bottom layer is full. Sprinkle with half the sugar and dot with butter. Repeat for the second layer. Cover and bake at 350° for 30 minutes. Serves 6.

Sybil La Budde

Cheese Grits

Grits are not just for tourist breakfasts down south. Serve these in place of potatoes.

1½ cups grits
5   cups salted water
¼   lb. butter or margarine
¾   lb. cheddar cheese, grated
3   eggs, beaten
½   cup milk
3   tsp. seasoned salt
½   tsp. garlic salt
2   tsp. paprika
dash hot pepper sauce

Cook grits in boiling salted water as directed on box. Add remaining ingredients. Pour into a 3-quart rectangular ovenproof dish. Bake at 350° for 40 to 60 minutes. Serves 8 to 10.

Marie Grayer

•

When Europeans first chanced upon the New World, native Americans had domesticated about 100 different plants. Many, such as corn, white potatoes, sweet potatoes and various kinds of beans, are staples in the world markets.

•

Notes

Salads and Dressings

Artifacts from East Africa

How much egg salad could be made from one ostrich egg? What would a vinaigrette made from palm nut oil taste like? Traveling with the museum's African Expedition fifty years ago would have given you the chance to find out. Weeks were spent on the Serengeti Plain and at the foot of Mt. Kilimanjaro collecting plants, animals and artifacts for museum exhibits.

The herders, hunters and agriculturalists of East Africa use a wide variety of material for their containers — wood, hide, fibers, and especially gourds. Besides edible crops, many gardens grow gourds, which when dried serve many purposes. Decorated with wood burning, beads, shells and the hides of wild animals, they are used for storage, decorations and musical instruments. Hide containers are used to churn butter and make a milk product similar to sour cream or yogurt. Ostrich shells carry water and are made into beads.

From left to right: Fiber bag (Kikuyu), Basket tray (Ikoma), Gourd rattles (Ikoma), Ostrich egg, Palm nut kernels, Ostrich shell beads (Ikoma), Hide butter churn (Turkana), Ivory snuff bottle (Nandi), Incised gourd container (Mbe), Incised gourd snuff bottle (Ikoma), Wood container (Turkana), Wood stool (Mbe), Gourd rattle (Giriami), Gourd container (Turkana) and beetle wing headpiece (Ikoma).

Salads & Dressings

Tomato and Green Bean Salad

2 lbs. fresh green beans
2 lbs. ripe tomatoes

dressing:
  4 Tbs. olive oil
  1 Tbs. wine vinegar
  1 Tbs. Worcestershire sauce
salt and pepper to taste

Cook beans in boiling water until just tender. Leave whole if young and slim. Chill. Peel tomatoes. Cut in eighths. Remove seeds and pulp. Pat dry with paper toweling. Combine dressing ingredients. Mix well. Mix vegetables with dressing. Chill at least 1 hour before serving. Serves 6 to 8.

Nina Hayssen

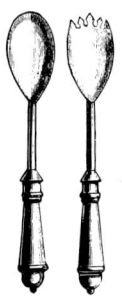

Cauliflower Salad

Add sliced black olives or chopped green peppers for more color, if you wish.

1 large cauliflower, cut into bite-sized pieces
1 cup chopped celery
½ cup chopped green onions
1 14-oz. can artichokes (water-packed), drained
1 cup Italian dressing
1 cup mayonnaise
4 Tbs. chili sauce
2 Tbs. lemon juice
2 tsp. dill weed
1 tsp. salt
parsley

Combine vegetables with Italian dressing. Marinate at least 6 hours or overnight. Drain. Combine the mayonnaise, chili sauce, lemon juice, dill weed and salt and mix well. Combine with the drained vegetables. Serve, garnished with parsley. Serves 10 to 12.

Sharon Goldstein

Salads & Dressings

Make-Ahead Salad

Add uncooked, thawed frozen peas if you want more color.

1 small head cauliflower, broken into pieces, about 3 cups
1 bunch broccoli, broken into pieces, about 5 cups
2 8-oz. cans water chestnuts, drained and sliced
1 8-oz. can sliced mushrooms, drained or 1 cup fresh, sliced
1 cup sour cream
1½ cups mayonnaise
1 pkg. original ranch-style buttermilk salad dressing mix

In a mixing bowl combine vegetables, tossing well to blend. In another bowl, combine remaining ingredients, mixing well. Pour over vegetables. Toss until well coated. May be made in the morning or the night before to blend flavors. Serves 8.

Harriet Vick

Marinated Vegies

Vary vegetables according to personal preferences or seasonal availability.

1 bunch carrots, peeled and cut on a diagonal ¼-inch thick
1 large head broccoli, broken into flowerettes
1 large white onion, peeled, quartered and separated
1 lb. fresh mushrooms, thinly sliced
½ head cauliflower, broken into flowerettes
½ head garlic, peeled, trimmed and mashed
4 stalks celery, cut on a diagonal ¼-inch thick
marinade:
⅔ cup safflower oil
⅓ cup tarragon vinegar
¼ cup burgundy wine
½ tsp. each basil and oregano
fresh ground pepper

In boiling unsalted water, blanch carrots, then broccoli. Simmer briefly for 3 minutes. Put into strainer. Immediately plunge into a large bowl of ice water to stop cooking process. Add more ice to keep water cool. In large earthenware or glass bowl, combine vegetables and marinade. Refrigerate several hours to blend flavors, stirring gently occasionally to coat vegetables. Remove garlic before serving. Serves 6 to 8.

Mary Garity

Salads & Dressings

Orange Jello Salad

A quick, easy recipe to make when time is short. For a large crowd, triple the recipe and place in a large ring mold.

1 3-oz. pkg. orange-flavored gelatin
1 cup hot water
1 cup white soda
1 small can crushed pineapple, drained
1 small can mandarin oranges, drained

Mix all ingredients together. Place in a mold. Refrigerate until set. Serves 6 to 8.

Sue Wettengel

Moroccan Vegetable Salad

Serve as a side dish or stuff into pita bread.

1 can garbanzo beans, rinsed and drained
½ lb. mushrooms, sliced (leave whole if small)
1 cup pitted black olives
2 green peppers, seeded and chopped
2 red peppers, seeded and chopped
12 cherry tomatoes

dressing:
1 cup yogurt
½ cup mayonnaise
2 cloves garlic, minced
2 Tbs. olive oil
1 Tbs. lemon juice
1 tsp. cumin
⅛ tsp. tumeric
salt and pepper

Steam mushrooms for 5 minutes. Drain and cool. Combine with remaining vegetables. Chill. Combine dressing ingredients. Mix well. Mix with vegetables. Chill 4 to 6 hours minimum. Serves 6 to 8.

Elizabeth Pleier

Salads & Dressings

Cranberry Orange Mold

A crowd pleaser or a family favorite.

2 6-oz. pkgs. cherry-flavored
    gelatin
2 cups hot water
2 cups sugar
1 8-oz. pkg. cranberries
1 or 2 apples
1 orange
½ cup chopped celery
½ cup chopped walnuts

Dissolve gelatin in hot water. Set aside to congeal to jelly thickness. Grind together the sugar, cranberries, apple and orange in food grinder. Add to congealed gelatin, stirring gently. Stir in celery and walnuts. Pour into 2-quart mold. Refrigerate. Unmold and decorate. Serves 12 to 14.

Marie Koenings

Molded Tuna Salad

A refreshing salad for a summer luncheon.

⅓ 10-oz. pkg. macaroni rings,
    cooked, rinsed and drained
½ cup minced celery
1 carrot, grated
3 hard-cooked eggs, chopped
1 7-oz. can tuna, flaked
1 medium onion, grated
½ cup mayonnaise
½ cup salad dressing
salt and pepper to taste
1 3-oz. pkg. lemon gelatin
1 Tbs. lemon juice
1½ cups boiling water

Combine macaroni, celery, carrot, eggs, tuna, mayonnaise, salad dressing, salt and pepper and mix well. Refrigerate. Combine gelatin with juice and water. Mix well. Let stand until somewhat firm. Whip until frothy. Fold in tuna mixture and pour into a mold. Chill until firm. Unmold and serve. Serves 6 to 8.

Bernice Simons

Salads & Dressings

Oriental Ode Salad

½ lb. spinach, washed and drained
1 cup bean sprouts
½ 6-oz. can water chestnuts,
    drained and cut in half
4 radishes, sliced

dressing:
    ¼ cup salad oil
    3 Tbs. sugar
    1½ Tbs. ketchup
    1 Tbs. plus 1 tsp. cider vinegar
    1 tsp. Worcestershire sauce
    ½ tsp. soy sauce
    1 Tbs. finely minced onion

Carefully tear spinach into bite-sized pieces. Wrap in paper towel to dry. Chill. Add bean sprouts, water chestnuts and radishes. In a small bowl, combine all the dressing ingredients. Beat well with a fork. Just before serving, combine the salad ingredients with the dressing. Serves 4.

Betty Peterson

Chicken Salad for Twenty

If served individually, mound salad on a crisp lettuce leaf. Top with almonds, a slice of green pepper and pineapple.

2 qts. (about 8 lbs.) coarsely cut up
    chicken or turkey breast meat
20 oz. water chestnuts, drained and
    sliced
2 lbs. seedless green grapes, halved
2 cups sliced celery
2 to 3 cups toasted slivered almonds

dressing:
    1 Tbs. curry powder
    2 Tbs. soy sauce
    3 cups mayonnaise
    2 Tbs. lemon juice
    pineapple slices

Cook meat until tender. Cool. Cut into bite-sized pieces. Combine chicken with water chestnuts. Add celery, grapes and 1½ cups almonds. Add dressing. Mix well. Chill several hours. Put into large serving bowl. Sprinkle on remaining almonds. Garnish with pineapple slices. Serves 20.

Marie Grayer

Salads & Dressings

Tortilla Chip Salad

1 lb. ground chuck
½ cup chopped celery
½ cup chopped green peppers
¾ cup chopped onion
garlic salt, chili powder and salt to taste
½ lb. process cheese
1 can tomatoes with green chilis
½ to ¾ head iceberg lettuce
2 tomatoes, quartered or cut in eighths
½ pkg. tortilla chips

Brown meat. Add celery, green pepper, onions and seasonings to taste. Cook for 10 minutes more. In a double boiler, melt the cheese. Add the tomatoes with chilis. Mix well. Put lettuce and tomatoes in a large bowl. Add crushed chips, hot meat mixture and cheese mixture. Mix well. Serve immediately. Serves 4 to Serves 4 to 5.

Sue Wettengel

Jellied Tomato Salad

An aspic type salad with a little body.

1   16-oz. can stewed tomatoes
1   3-oz. pkg. lemon gelatin
1   tsp. vinegar or lemon juice

Stir gelatin and lemon juice into tomatoes. Bring to a boil and cook for 1 minute. Spoon mixture into 4 individual molds or 1 large one or return to the tomato can. Chill. If can is used, open bottom and push out contents. Serve with a garnish of greens and mayonnaise or Green Goddess type dressing. Serves 4.

Mildred Booth

•

Tomatoes were eaten by the Indians but to Europe and the New World it was an ornamental plant, though once accepted it became very popular. It was and sometimes is called the "love apple" from the saying, "If the tomato doesn't poison you, it will make you fall in love."

•

138

Salads & Dressings

Crab Louis

Shrimp can be substituted for this quick and easy yet elegant dish.

¾ cup mayonnaise
¼ cup ketchup
2 Tbs. sweet pickle relish, drained
1 Tbs. lemon juice
½ small head iceberg lettuce
2 tomatoes, cut in wedges
1 cucumber, sliced
½ lb. crabmeat, cut into 1-inch
   pieces
3 hard-boiled eggs, sliced
paprika
black olives, optional

Blend together mayonnaise, ketchup, pickle relish and lemon juice. Chill several hours before using. Prepare a bed of lettuce on serving platter. Salt sparingly. Arrange tomatoes, cucumber and crabmeat on lettuce. Pour sauce over all. Attractively arrange egg slices over sauce and dust lightly with paprika. Garnish with olives. Serves 4.

Beverly Jaeger

Marinated Vegetable Salad

1 can peas, drained
1 can whole green beans, drained
1 small jar chopped pimiento,
   drained
1 small bunch celery hearts,
   chopped
1 green pepper, seeded and
   chopped
1 medium onion, chopped

dressing:
1½ cups sugar
1 cup cider vinegar
1 cup salad oil
1 tsp. paprika
salt

Combine vegetables in a bowl. Beat or shake dressing ingredients in a jar to mix well. Pour over vegetables. Marinate at least 24 hours in refrigerator, stirring gently several times to coat well. Serves 6.

Elizabeth Pleier

Salads & Dressings

Cucumber DeLuxe Salad

A molded salad with a crunch to it.

1 3-oz. pkg. lime-flavored gelatin
1 cup hot water
2 heaping Tbs. salad dressing
1 cup small-curd cottage cheese, drained
1 cup minced celery
2 Tbs. minced onion
1/3 cup peeled, finely-chopped cucumber

Combine gelatin with hot water. Mix until dissolved. Add salad dressing, mixing well with a whisk. Add remaining ingredients, mixing well. Put into a ring mold. Refrigerate until firm. Serves 6 to 8.

Sue Wettengel

Shrimp and Avocado Salad

3 lbs. fresh or frozen shrimp
1 Tbs. shrimp spice
1/4 Tbs. tarragon vinegar
2 tsp. grated onion
2 tsp. salt
1 tsp. white pepper
1/2 tsp. dry mustard
2 sprigs fresh dill
1/2 cup vegetable oil
3 avocados
lemon juice
lettuce

dressing:
1/2 cup sour cream
1 Tbs. lemon juice
2 tsp. prepared horseradish
1 tsp. finely cut dill

Tie the shrimp spice in cheesecloth. Cook with the shrimp in boiling salt water for 5 minutes or until shrimp turn pink. Drain. Plunge into cold water. Shell and devein the shrimp. Combine the lemon juice, vinegar, onion, salt, pepper, mustard, dill and oil. Pour over shrimp. Marinate overnight in refrigerator. Halve, pit and peel avocados. Slice into rings. Sprinkle with lemon juice to prevent discoloration. Drain shrimp. Arrange alternating layers of shrimp and avocado on a bed of lettuce. Combine dressing ingredients and pour over salad. Serves 6.

Jo Ann Beightol

140

Salads & Dressings

Mandarin Orange Sherbet Salad

A molded salad that will add color to a buffet table. Fresh orange juice can be substituted for some of the water or use lemon-flavored gelatin instead of orange.

2   3-oz. pkgs. orange-flavored
    gelatin
2   cups boiling water
1   small can mandarin oranges,
    including juice
1   pt. orange sherbet

Dissolve gelatin in hot water. Add remaining ingredients in order listed, mixing well. Place in a mold. Refrigerate until set, preferably overnight. Unmold. Decorate or serve as you wish. Serves 10 to 12.

Marie Koenings

Cranberry-Tuna Mold

1   envelope unflavored gelatin
¼   cup cold water
¼   cup boiling water
2   7-oz. cans water-packed tuna
1   cup mayonnaise
1   cup chopped celery
1   small onion, chopped

topping:
    1   3-oz. pkg. lemon-flavored
        gelatin
    ¾   cup boiling water
    1   can whole cranberry sauce
    ¼   cup orange juice

Soften gelatin in cold water. Add boiling water, stirring to dissolve. Add tuna, mayonnaise, celery and onion. Mix well. Spoon into an 8x8-inch mold. Chill until firm. For topping, dissolve gelatin in boiling water. Add sauce and juice. Mix well. Spoon over tuna mixture. Chill overnight. Serves 8.

Dorothy Dreher

Salads & Dressings

Spinach Salad

1 lb. spinach, washed, dried,
   torn into bite-sized pieces
2 hard-cooked eggs
1 large apple, diced
1 small onion, sliced
¼ lb. blue cheese, crumbled
½ cup mayonnaise
½ cup sour cream
salt and pepper to taste

Refrigerate spinach until serving time. Combine remaining ingredients. Add to spinach just before serving and toss. Serves 4 to 6.

Phyllis Reimer

Beef Salad Parisienne

A salad that also could be garnished with thinly sliced pickled walnuts, chopped parsley or hard-cooked egg wedges.

2 cups boiled new potatoes, sliced
   or cubed
1 cup green onions, finely sliced
2 cups celery hearts with tops,
   chopped
3 cups cooked lean beef, sliced into
   small strips or diced
8 to 10 midget dill pickles, sliced
1 cup cherry tomatoes, halved
¼ cup capers, rinsed in cold water,
   drained
½ cup thin green pepper strips

dressing:
   3 hard-cooked egg yolks,
      mashed, reserving whites
   3 Tbs. Dijon mustard
   1 cup oil
   1 clove garlic, minced with ¼ tsp.
   salt
   1 tsp. freshly ground pepper
   ⅓ cup vinegar
   dash hot pepper sauce
salad greens

Combine salad ingredients in a large bowl. Beat together dressing ingredients. Pour over vegetables. Marinate at least 8 hours or overnight. Bring to room temperature to serve. Arrange on salad greens. Garnish with chopped egg whites. Serves 6 to 8.

Elizabeth Pleier

142

Salads & Dressings

Westport Salad

Dressing, which keeps for weeks refrigerated, improves in flavor if made ahead.

romaine and iceberg lettuce
½ head cauliflower, cut into small pieces
1 to 2 cups buttered bread crumbs

dressing:
1 clove garlic, pressed
1 cup salad dressing
2 Tbs. grated parmesan cheese
1 Tbs. lemon juice
sour or regular cream

Tear romaine and iceberg into bite-sized pieces. In a large salad bowl, combine romaine, lettuce and cauliflower. Top with bread crumbs. To make dressing, combine all ingredients, thinning with sour cream. At serving time, add dressing to lettuce mixture. Toss. Serves 8.

Marie Grayer

Bonhomme Salmon Salad

2 envelopes unflavored gelatin
½ cup cold water
1 16-oz. can red salmon, drained, saving liquid
½ cup finely chopped celery
¼ cup finely chopped onion
½ cup ketchup
¼ cup vinegar
1 cup mayonnaise

Soften gelatin in water. Flake and mix salmon with celery and onion. Combine reserved salmon liquid, ketchup and vinegar in a saucepan. Boil. Stir in gelatin until dissolved. Blend in salmon mixture. Stir in mayonnaise. Chill. If a fish mold is used, when turned out, decorate with sliced olives for eyes and thinly sliced radishes for fish scales, using a bit of mayonnaise for "glue." Serves 8.

Peg Nelson

Salads & Dressings

Oriental Salad

1 head iceberg lettuce, shredded
1 cup diced celery
4 green onions, chopped
3 Tbs. minced parsley
1 11-oz. can mandarin oranges
1 small pkg. sliced almonds, toasted

dressing:
    4 Tbs. vinegar
    ½ cup salad oil
    4 Tbs. sugar
    1 tsp. salt

In a large bowl, combine lettuce, celery, onions, parsley and oranges. Combine dressing ingredients. Mix well. Toss with lettuce mixture. Place onto individual serving plates. Top with almonds. Serves 6 to 8.

Lydia Kniephoff

•

There basically are two kinds of almonds—bitter and sweet. We eat the sweet variety; the bitter are used for almond flavoring after being processed first to remove prussic acid, a poison.

•

Caesar Salad

An easy version of a classic that looks and tastes spectacular. Dressing can be made at least a week in advance.

1 egg
¾ cup salad oil
¼ cup lemon juice
1 tsp. salt
1 Tbs. Worcestershire sauce
1 tsp. black pepper
⅛ tsp. garlic powder
¼ cup parmesan cheese
croutons
2 heads romaine lettuce

Put egg in boiling water for 1 minute. Beat in a blender until light. Add salad oil and lemon juice gradually, beating at low speed until foamy. Add salt, Worcestershire sauce, pepper, garlic powder and cheese and mix at low speed. Refrigerate until ready to use. Mix croutons with bite-sized pieces of romaine. Toss with dressing. Serves 8 to 10.

Bobbe Blumberg

Salads & Dressings

Tossed Greens and Grapefruit Salad

A good salad to serve with spicy foods. It is tart and crunchy.

1 cup fresh grapefruit segments
½ cup seeded sliced cucumber
½ cup diced green and red pepper
1 small, sweet onion, sliced
mixed greens

dressing:
   1 Tbs. lemon juice
   3 Tbs. salad oil
   ½ tsp. dry mustard
   dash garlic salt
   salt and pepper to taste

Combine salad ingredients in a large bowl. Chill until serving time. Combine dressing ingredients. Mix well. Pour over salad at serving time and toss. Serves 4.

Elizabeth Pleier

Carrot Sunflower Salad

2 cups grated carrots
½ cup hulled sunflower seeds
3 green onions, chopped fine
garlic powder to taste
½ cup mayonnaise
lettuce or other greens
1 medium tomato, cut into thin wedges

Combine carrots, seeds, onion and garlic powder in a bowl. Add mayonnaise. Blend well. Place washed lettuce or greens in a serving bowl. Spoon on carrot mixture. Surround with tomato wedges. Serve chilled. Serves 4 to 6.

Judy De Vries

Salads & Dressings

Greek Garden Salad

2 heads romaine, coarsely
   shredded
1 bunch green onions, chopped
1 small onion (Red Italian
   preferred), sliced
4 radishes, sliced
½ small cucumber, peeled and
   sliced
12 black olives (Greek preferred),
   pitted
½ to 1 cup feta cheese, rinsed and
   crumbled
12 cherry tomatoes, halved
¼ tsp. oregano
juice of 2 lemons
6 to 8 Tbs. oil (part olive oil)
freshly ground pepper

Combine first 9 ingredients, mixing
well. Add lemon juice. Toss. Add oil.
Toss again. Add pepper to taste.
Serves 8 to 10.

Elizabeth Pleier

Broccoli Parisian

This may well become a family
favorite.

1 bunch, about 2 lbs., fresh broccoli
⅓ cup parsley, chopped
1 clove garlic, crushed
1½ tsp. salt
⅓ cup olive or vegetable oil
¼ cup tarragon or cider vinegar
1 Tbs. prepared mustard
1 hard-cooked egg, sliced

Trim leaves and wash broccoli. Split
stems and slice into bite-sized pieces
(makes about 6 cups). Drain well.
Combine remaining ingredients,
except egg, in a large bowl, preferably glass. Add broccoli. Toss and
coat well .Garnish with egg slices.
Serves 6 to 8.

Julie Revane

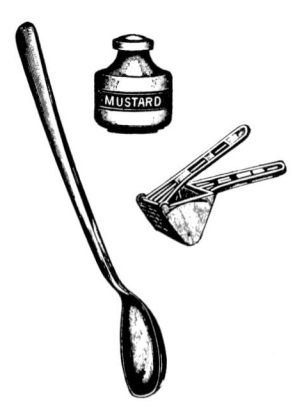

Salads & Dressings

Raw Spinach Salad

4 cups chopped fresh spinach
¾ cup diced cheddar cheese
½ cup chopped celery
½ cup chopped green onion
3 hard-cooked eggs, sliced

dressing:
  1½ cups mayonnaise
  ¼ cup prepared mustard
  1½ tsp. cider vinegar
  ½ tsp. salt

Combine all salad ingredients in a salad bowl. Eggs can be reserved for topping, if preferred. Combine dressing ingredients. Mix well. Add to spinach mixture, tossing well to coat. Serves 4.

Marie Grayer

Spinach-Avocado Salad

1 lb. spinach, cleaned and stemmed
1 or 2 avocados, cut into wedges

dressing:
  ¼ cup chablis
  ½ tsp. dry mustard
  2 egg yolks
  ½ cup oil
  ¾ Tbs. lemon juice
  dash of sugar
  dash of salt
  ½ Tbs. chopped fresh chives or parsley

Combine wine and mustard. Let stand 15 minutes. Add egg yolks and whisk in. Add oil gradually, beating constantly. When dressing is thick, add remaining ingredients, beating well. Pour over spinach and avocados. Other fruits, such as strawberries, seedless grapes or cantalope may be used. Serves 8.

Elizabeth Pleier

Salads & Dressings

French Dressing

A versatile recipe. Use it on salads, as a marinade for beef, or as a sauce for beef fondue.

¾ cup salad oil
⅔ cup sugar (or less)
⅔ cup tomato ketchup
¼ cup cider vinegar
1 tsp. steak sauce
1 tsp. paprika
1 tsp. garlic salt or 1 tsp. salt and 1 tsp. grated onion

Beat all ingredients together in a mixer for 10 minutes. Yields 2 cups.

Mitzi Halkerston

Elsie's Blue Cheese Dressing

1 cup oil
⅔ cup ketchup
¼ cup cider vinegar
⅔ cup sugar
juice of 1 lemon
dash of salt
1 tsp. paprika
1 clove garlic, minced
crumbled blue cheese

Mix together all ingredients except cheese. Serve on tossed salad greens. Top with cheese. Yields 2 cups.

Elizabeth Pleier

Bavarian Salad Dressing

Serve this over tossed vegetable salad (greens, tomatoes, cucumbers, celery, onions).

1 cup salad oil
½ cup cider vinegar
½ cup sugar
juice of 1 lemon
1 small onion, grated
fresh ground pepper
dash of cayenne pepper
dash of celery salt
¾ cup tomato ketchup

Mix all ingredients together in a jar and shake. Allow to stand at least 12 hours before using to improve flavor. Yields 2 cups.

Bernice Simons

Notes

Desserts and Sweets

European 19th century decorative and utilitarian wares

In the back row, a wheel-cut and gilded cordial glass from France, 1890; an 8½" ivory carving of an 18th century couple walking, mounted on a gilt silver repoisse stand, from France, 1800-1820; and a clam's broth Bristol glass garniture vase decorated with enamel and gold, Hodgetts, Richardson & Son, Stourbridge, England, 1870.

The middle row is part of a porcelain tea set with lustrous glaze and gilding produced by Helena Wolfsohn of Dresden, Germany, which won a gold medal at the World's Columbian Exposition in Chicago in 1892. In the front is another plate designed by Helena Wolfsohn in the same time period.

Desserts & Sweets

Mrs. Mac's Eggnog Pie

An old, southern recipe. Garnish with shaved chocolate.

1   9-inch baked pie shell
4   egg yolks, slightly beaten
½   cup sugar
½   tsp. salt
½   cup hot water
1   envelope unflavored gelatin
½   cup cold water
4   egg whites, stiffly beaten
½   cup sugar
1   tsp. nutmeg
4   Tbs. rum or bourbon whiskey
½   pt. heavy cream, whipped

Combine egg yolks, sugar, salt and hot water. Cook over boiling water until mixture coats a spoon, stirring constantly. Dissolve gelatin in cold water. Pour egg mixture over gelatin. Blend well. Cool. When mixture starts to congeal, fold in the beaten egg whites, sugar, nutmeg, rum or bourbon. Pour into pie shell. Cover with whipped cream. Chill. Serves 6 to 8.

Peg Nelson

Derby Pie

A very sweet dessert which can be served with whipped cream, un-sweetened. Add 1 or 2 tablespoons of bourbon, if you wish.

3   eggs
1   cup light brown sugar
1   cup light corn syrup
¼   tsp. salt
½   cup margarine, melted
1   tsp. vanilla
½   cup English walnuts, chopped
½   cup chocolate bits
1   10-inch pie shell, unbaked

Combine first 6 ingredients. Mix well. Fold in the nuts and chocolate. Pour into the unbaked pie shell. Bake at 350° for 50 minutes. Serves 8 to 10.

Dorothy Dreher

153

Desserts & Sweets

Cheesecake Pie

1¼ cups graham cracker crumbs
¼ cup melted butter
1 8-oz. pkg. cream cheese,
  softened
½ cup sugar
1 Tbs. lemon juice
½ tsp. vanilla
dash of salt
2 eggs
1 cup sour cream
2 Tbs. sugar
1 tsp. vanilla

Combine crumbs and butter. Press into an 8-inch pie plate. Beat cream cheese until fluffy. Gradually blend in sugar, lemon juice, vanilla and salt. Add eggs, one at a time, beating well after each. Pour filling into crust. Bake at 325° for 25 to 30 minutes, or until set. Combine sour cream, sugar and vanilla. Spread over top of pie. Bake 10 minutes longer. Cool. Chill several hours. Serves 6 to 8.

Marian Miller

Kentucky Fudge Pie

A wickedly rich pie, full of calories, but a chocolate lovers delight!

1 9-inch baked pie shell
½ cup butter, softened
¾ cup sugar
2 squares bitter chocolate, melted
1 tsp. vanilla
2 eggs
whipped cream

Cream the butter. Gradually add the sugar. Cream well. Blend in the melted, cooled chocolate and vanilla. Add the egg, one at a time. Beat 5 minutes after each egg is added. Turn into the cooled pie crust. Chill for at least 4 hours. Top with whipped cream. Serves 6 to 8.

Ann Hill

•

Homemade pies were a favorite dish in colonial homes. When fruit was plentiful in the fall, a great many pies would be made, then frozen in an outdoor shed. A pie then could be thawed in the warming cupboard above the fireplace when it was served.

•

Desserts & Sweets

Ritz Cracker Pie

Results taste almost like a meringue with nuts.

3 egg whites
1 tsp. baking powder
1 cup sugar
20 Ritz crackers, rolled fine
½ cup chopped walnuts or pecans
1 tsp. vanilla
whipped cream for topping
fruit of your choice (fresh strawberries, raspberries, sliced peaches or kiwi fruit)

Beat egg whites until stiff. Add baking powder. Gradually add sugar. Fold in cracker crumbs. Add nuts and vanilla. Put into a 9-inch greased pie pan. Bake at 325° for 30 minutes. Cool. Top with whipped cream. Refrigerate. At serving time, top with fruit. Serves 6 or 7.

Mildred Booth

Refrigerator Lime Pie

1 9-inch graham cracker pie shell
1½ tsp. unflavored gelatin
⅓ cup cold water
4 eggs, separated
⅓ cup lime juice
1 tsp. grated lime rind
1 cup sugar
⅛ tsp. salt
green food coloring
½ pt. heavy cream, whipped

Soften gelatin in water. In a double boiler, beat egg yolks slightly. Add juice, rind and ½ cup sugar. Cook over boiling water until mixture coats a spoon. Remove from heat. Add softened gelatin. Beat egg whites until stiff. Beat in remaining sugar. Fold into egg yolk mixture. Add food coloring for desired color. Pour into pie shell. Chill. Serve with whipped cream. Serves 6 to 8.

Mary Zastrow

Desserts & Sweets

Peaches and Cream Pie

1   8-inch pie crust
6   large peaches, peeled and sliced
½   cup sugar
3   Tbs. flour
¼   to ½ tsp. cinnamon
¾   cup cream (half-and-half or part
      whipping cream for added rich
      ness)

Arrange peaches in a pastry-lined pan. Combine remaining ingredients. Mix well. Pour over peaches. Bake at 375° for 40 to 45 minutes. Serves 8.

Harriette Vick

Cranberry Pie

For variety, blueberries, apples or rhubarb may be used instead of cranberries.

2   cups cranberries
1½ cups sugar
2   eggs, well beaten
½   cup chopped nuts
1   cup flour
½   cup butter, melted

Spread berries in a greased 9 or 10-inch round pan. Sprinkle with nuts and ½ cup sugar. Combine eggs with 1 cup sugar. Beat well. Add flour and butter. Beat well. Spread over berry mixture. Bake at 325° for 1 hour. Serves 8.

Sharon Roderick

Mocha Ice Cream Pie

20 coconut bar cookies, crushed
¼   cup butter, softened
¼   cup brown sugar
1   pt. coffee ice cream, softened
      slightly
shaved milk chocolate

Combine the cookie crumbs, butter and brown sugar. Mix well. Line a 7-inch square pan with the crumb mixture, saving some for topping. Spread softened ice cream over crumbs. Sprinkle with chocolate and reserved crumb mixture. Cover with foil and freeze. Soften slightly before serving. Serves 8.

Carol Dickson

Desserts & Sweets

Pineapple Cheese Tarts

*3   8-oz. pkgs. cream cheese,
   softened
²/₃ cup sugar
3   eggs
1   tsp. vanilla
1   20-oz. can crushed pineapple,
   drained
24 vanilla wafers*

Whip first four ingredients together until light and fluffy. Add ¼ cup pineapple. Place a vanilla wafer into paper-lined cupcake tins, 2½ inches in diameter. Pour cheese mixture over wafer, filling ²/₃ full. Bake at 350° for 15 minutes. When cool, top with remaining crushed pineapple. Refrigerate. Yields 24 tarts.

Patricia Dulski

Cherry Cheese Tarts

A colorful, flavorful and quick recipe.

*3   8-oz. pkgs. cream cheese,
   softened
²/₃ cup sugar
3   eggs
1   tsp. vanilla
¼   cup cottage cheese (optional)
24 vanilla wafers
1   20-oz. can cherry pie filling*

Whip first 5 ingredients together until light and fluffy. Place a vanilla wafer into paper-lined cupcake tins, 2½ inches in diameter. Pour cheese mixture over wafer, filling ²/₃ full. Bake at 350° for 15 minutes. When cool, top with cherry pie filling. Yields 24 tarts.

Patricia Dulski

Desserts & Sweets

Orange Ice Box Cake

A light and delicate dessert. Would be nice served after a summer meal. Sponge cake can be made ahead and frozen.

cake:
- 4 eggs, separated
- 1 cup sugar
- 5 Tbs. water
- ¼ tsp. salt
- ½ tsp. vanilla
- 1 cup cake flour
- 2 tsp. baking powder

filling:
- ½ cup sugar
- 1 Tbs. cornstarch
- 3 eggs, separated
- 1 Tbs. butter
- 1 cup orange juice
- rind of 1 orange, grated
- 1 cup heavy cream, whipped

To make cake, beat egg yolks until thick and lemon colored. Gradually add sugar, water, salt and vanilla. Fold in flour sifted with baking powder. Beat egg whites until stiff. Fold into batter. Pour into 2 9-inch cake pans which have been greased and lined with wax paper. Bake at 350° for 25 minutes. Turn out of pans. Place on rack to cool. Split each layer in half. To make filling, blend sugar and cornstarch together. Add the well-beaten egg yolk, butter, juice and rind. Cook in a double boiler until thick. Cool. Beat the egg whites until stiff. Fold in the whipped cream. Add to the cooled custard. Blend well. Spread the mixture between the layers and over the cake. Refrigerate at least 6 hours or overnight. Serves 10 to 12.

Carol Dugan

Desserts & Sweets

Three Hole Cake

1½ cups flour
1 cup sugar
1 tsp. baking soda
3 to 4 Tbs. cocoa
1 tsp. salt
1 Tbs. vinegar
⅓ cup cooking oil
1 tsp. vanilla
1 cup water

lazy daisy topping:
  ⅔ cup brown sugar
  6 Tbs. margarine
  1⅓ cups shredded coconut
  ⅓ cup milk

Combine the flour, sugar, baking soda, cocoa and salt in an 8-inch square pan or 9-inch loaf pan. Mix well. Make three wells in flour mixture. Put vinegar in one well, oil in second well and vanilla in third well. Pour water over entire mixture. Stir all together with a fork, mixing well. Bake at 350° for 30 minutes.
To make topping, cream together the brown sugar and margarine. Add the coconut and milk. Mix well. Spread over cake. Place under broiler for a few minutes until top becomes bubbly and light brown. Cake may also be sprinkled with powdered sugar or frosted with you favorite powdered sugar icing.
Serves 9 to 12.

Judy De Vries

Special Date Nut Cake

1 cup pitted and cut up dates
1 tsp. baking soda
1 cup hot water
1 Tbs. butter, softened
1 egg
1 tsp. vanilla
1¼ cups flour
1 tsp. baking powder
¼ tsp. salt
1 cup nuts

Combine the dates, soda and water. Let stand for ½ hour. Blend together the butter, egg and vanilla. Add the date mixture. Sift together the dry ingredients. Add to date mixture with the nuts. Mix well. Pour into a 9x9-inch pan. Bake at 325° for 30 minutes. Serve with ice cream or powdered sugar. Serves 9.

Jean Lindemann

Desserts & Sweets

Excellent Spice Cake

½ cup butter
2 cups brown sugar
1 egg
2 cups flour
1 tsp. baking soda
½ tsp. ground cloves
1 tsp. cinnamon
¼ tsp. nutmeg
½ cup chopped walnuts
1 cup raisins
1 cup sour milk (add 1 Tbs. vinegar
   to 1 cup milk)

Cream together the butter and brown sugar. Add the egg. Beat well. Combine the remaining ingredients, except the milk. Mix together well. Add to the creamed mixture, alternating with the sour milk. Pour into a 9x13-inch pan or into cupcake tins. Bake at 350° for 25 to 30 minutes. If desired, frost sparingly with a butter cream frosting. Serves 9 to 12, or makes about 2 dozen cupcakes.

Jane Houston

Aunt Anna's Cream Cheese Cake

Serve small slices as it is a rich dessert.

14 slices zwieback. rolled fine
2 Tbs. sugar
3 Tbs. butter, softened
2 16-oz. pkgs. cream cheese,
   softened
1 cup heavy sour cream
½ tsp. salt
2 tsp. lemon juice or 1 tsp. lemon
   juice and 1 tsp. vanilla
1½ tsp. grated lemon rind
6 Tbs. sifted flour
4 eggs, well beaten
1 cup sugar

Grease bottom and sides of a 9-inch spring form with 1 tablespoon butter. Combine zwieback, sugar and 2 tablespoons of butter. Mix well. Press evenly on bottom and sides of pan, reserving ½ cup of the crumb mixture for topping. Combine the cream cheese, sour cream, salt, juice, rind and flour. Mix well. Add the eggs and sugar, stirring until smooth. Pour into pan. Sprinkle with the reserved crumbs. Bake at 325° for 1 hour or until almost firm in the center. Turn off heat. Open oven door. Leave ajar another hour. Remove from oven. Let cool. Then refrigerate. Serves 18.

Joan Brengel

160

Desserts & Sweets

Decadent Devil's Food Cake

A cake made from a mix that tastes as if it was imported from Europe.

1   18½-oz. pkg. devil's food cake mix
1   6-oz. pkg. semisweet chocolate chips
½   cup rum
½   cup apricot preserves

frosting:
1   6-oz. pkg. semisweet chocolate chips
1   cup sour cream
¼   tsp. salt

Prepare cake mix as directed. Stir in chocolate chips. Spoon into 2 greased 9-inch cake pans. Bake at 350° for 30 to 35 minutes. Cool 5 minutes on wire rack. Remove from pans. Brush tops with rum. Let cool. Spread one layer with preserves. To make frosting, melt chocolate chips in a double boiler. Remove from heat. Stir in sour cream and salt. Beat until smooth and creamy. Assemble layers. Spread frosting on top and sides. Serves 10 to 12.

Bobbe Blumberg

Pineapple Cake with Ginger Frosting

Rich, moist and chunky. Similar to a carrot cake.

2   eggs
1   20-oz. can crushed pineapple, undrained
2   cups all-purpose flour
1   cup sugar
1   cup brown sugar
2   tsp. baking soda
1   cup chopped walnuts

frosting:
3   oz. cream cheese, softened
4   Tbs. butter or margarine
1   tsp. vanilla
2   cups powdered sugar
½   tsp. ground ginger

In a large bowl, beat the eggs until light and fluffy. Add pineapple, flour, sugars, and baking soda. Mix by hand to avoid too much air in batter. Stir in nuts. Spread evenly in an ungreased 9x13-inch baking dish. Bake at 350° for 45 to 50 minutes or until an inserted toothpick comes out clean. Cool. Beat together the cream cheese, butter and vanilla using an electric mixer. Gradually add the sugar and ginger, beating until smooth. Spread on cooled cake. Yields 16 to 18.

Dolores Dornoff

Harvey Wallbanger Cake

A moist cake that keeps for days. Recipe includes directions for homemade Galliano.

1 pkg. orange supreme cake mix
1   3-oz. pkg. instant vanilla pudding
4 eggs
½ cup corn oil
¾ cup orange juice
¼ cup vodka
¼ cup Galliano, commercial or homemade

topping:
1 cup powdered sugar
1½ Tbs. orange juice
1½ Tbs. vodka
1½ Tbs. Galliano, commercial or homemade

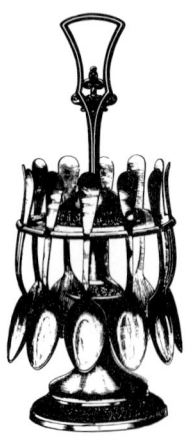

Mix together the cake mix and pudding mix. Set aside. Blend together the eggs, oil, juice, vodka and Galliano. Slowly add the liquid mixture to the cake mix mixture while beating for 4 to 5 minutes with an electric mixer. Pour into a 10-inch angel food pan. Bake at 350° for 45 to 55 minutes. Let cool in pan right side up. Mix topping ingredients together. Drizzle over top of cake which has been removed from pan.

To make homemade Galliano, mix 2 cups sugar with ¾ cup water. Boil and cool. Add 3 teaspoons vanilla, ½ teaspoon anise extract, 3 teaspoons lemon or lime juice, 4 drops yellow food coloring and 2½ cups vodka. Stir until thoroughly mixed. Strain into a clean, empty liquor bottle. Let stand for 2 weeks, shaking frequently to prevent any settling. Serves 10 to 12.

Marie Koenings

Desserts & Sweets

Adam and Eve Torte

¼ cup butter
1 cup sugar
1 egg
1 cup flour
1 tsp. baking soda
¼ tsp. nutmeg
¼ tsp. cinnamon
2 cups chopped apples
¼ cup chopped nuts

topping:
    ½ cup brown sugar
    ¼ cup sugar
    ½ tsp. vanilla
    ½ cup half and half
    ½ cup butter

Cream together the butter and sugar. Add remaining ingredients. Pour into a greased 7x12-inch pan. Bake at 350° for 40 minutes. Combine topping ingredients. Simmer 5 minutes. Serve warm over cake topping with ice cream. Serves 12.

Carol Tishler

Ice Cream Torte

For variety, use different ice cream and pudding flavors.

1 cup crushed graham crackers
1 cup crushed soda crackers
1 stick margarine, melted
½ gal. butter pecan ice cream, softened
1 cup milk
2 3¾-oz. pkgs. instant French vanilla pudding
whipped cream

Combine both cracker crumbs with margarine. Press into 9x13-inch pan. May be baked a little to firm up. Combine remaining ingredients, except whipping cream. Mix well with electric mixer. Pour into crust. Top with whipped cream. Chill at least 12 hours or overnight. Add nuts when using vanilla ice cream. Top with hot fudge sauce. Serves 8 to 12.

Phyllis Weis

163

Desserts & Sweets

Colonial Apple Torte

Original recipe is from an 1800 s cookbook. Serve hot or cold, with whipped cream, ice cream, cheese slice or lemon sauce.

6 to 8 apples, peeled and sliced
1 cup sugar
1 tsp. cinnamon
1 cup packed dark or light brown sugar, or ½ cup of each
1 cup [scant] flour
¾ stick butter, softened
1 tsp. vanilla extract
1 cup chopped nuts

Fill a 9x13-inch baking dish with the apples. Press down firmly. Combine the sugar with the cinnamon. Sprinkle over apples. Combine the brown sugar with the flour. Cut the butter into the sugar-flour mixture. Add the vanilla and nuts. Mix well. Spread over the apples. Press level with a fork. Bake at 350° for 1 hour. Serves 10 to 12.

Elizabeth Thier

•

Sugar was a luxury item in colonial times because it was imported from the Indies. Settlers learned from the Indians how to tap maple trees for syrup. When the syrup was thick enough it was hardened and allowed to crystallize into sugar as a household sweetener.

•

Cherry-Berry Torte

2 cups flour
1 cup butter, softened
3 Tbs. sugar
1 16-oz. can tart cherries, drained, reserving juice
1 10-oz. pkg. frozen strawberries, thawed and drained, reserving juice
1 cup sugar
2 Tbs. cornstarch
2 Tbs. tapioca
1 Tbs. lemon juice
dash of salt

Combine flour, butter and sugar. Mix well. Press into a 9x13-inch pan. Bake at 400° for 10 to 15 minutes or until golden. Combine the reserved juices with the sugar, cornstarch, tapioca, juice and salt. Cook over medium heat, stirring constantly, until thick, about 8 minutes. Cool. Add cherries and strawberries. Pour over baked "muerbeteig." Refrigerate. Serve with whipped cream. Serves 12.

Lydia Kniephoff

Desserts & Sweets

Bess Truman's Brownies

Recipe is from Mrs. Harry S. Truman who taught submitter how to make these when a 10-year-old girl. Easy for young children to make, with a fluffy appearance and rich, dark, chewy center.

¾ cup flour
6 Tbs. cocoa
1 cup sugar
½ cup butter or shortening
2 eggs
1 cup chopped pecans
1 tsp. vanilla

Sift together the flour and cocoa. Add remaining ingredients. Mix well. Spoon into an 8x8-inch pan. Bake at 350° for 20 minutes or until an inserted toothpick comes out clean. Cut into squares. Yields 16.

Marie Grayer

Spicy Refrigerator Cookies

1 cup butter
½ cup sugar
½ cup light brown sugar
1 egg
2¼ cups sifted flour
½ tsp. baking soda
½ tsp. salt
2 tsp. cinnamon
¼ tsp. nutmeg
¼ tsp. ground cloves
½ cup finely chopped nuts

Cream together the butter, both sugars and egg. Sift together the dry ingredients. Add the nuts. Add to creamed mixture. Beat well. Shape into 4 rolls about 2 inches in diameter. Wrap in wax paper. Chill thoroughly. Slice into 1/8-inch thick pieces. Place on cookie sheets. Bake at 375° for 5 to 7 minutes. Yields 6 to 7 dozen.

Jane Houston

Desderts & Sweets

'Nilla Orange Balls

Serve these with a dish of ice cream or on any cookie tray.

1 12-oz. box vanilla wafers, crushed
1 cup ground pecans
1 stick of butter, melted
1 cup packed powdered sugar
1 6-oz. can frozen orange concentrate, thawed

Mix all ingredients together well. Refrigerate until easy to form into balls. Roll into balls using a teaspoon measure to scoop out dough. Roll in additional powdered sugar. Refrigerate until ready to serve. If desired, reroll in powdered sugar before serving. Keeps well for days refrigerated. Yields 5 to 6 dozen balls.

Arlene Mann

Lemon Macaroons

An easy to make, rich cookie coconut lovers will enjoy. Glazed cherries may be difficult to find in some stores in some months.

2/3 cup sweetened condensed milk
1/4 cup bottled lemon juice
1 7-oz. pkg. flaked coconut
1 4-oz. pkg. glazed cherries, chopped

Combine the milk and juice. Milk will thicken. Add the coconut and cherries. Mix well. Form into 1-inch balls. Place on a well-oiled cookie sheet or drop by teaspoonfuls, 2 inches apart. Bake at 300° for 30 minutes, until slightly brown, checking during baking time. Yield 2½ dozen.

Dorothy Dreher

Desserts & Sweets

Pearl Baldwin's Melted Moment Cookies

½ lb. butter
5½ Tbs. powdered sugar
¾ cup cornstarch
1 cup flour

glaze:
   1 cup powdered sugar
   1 Tbs. butter
   1 Tbs. lemon juice

Cream butter and sugar together. Add cornstarch and flour. Mix well. Chill slightly. Form into walnut-sized balls. Place on a cookie sheet. Flatten with the bottom of a glass dipped in sugar. Bake at 350° for 10 to 12 minutes, until golden brown around edges. Beat together glaze ingredients. Glaze cookies while still warm, keeping glaze soft to avoid breaking delicate cookies. Yields 3 dozen.

Cava Ross

Mazurki (Strawberry Cookies)

2 sticks margarine
2 cups flour
2 eggs
⅓ cup sugar
10 oz. strawberry jam
1 cup sugar
4 eggs
2 cups chopped walnuts
1 tsp. vanilla

Combine margarine and flour. Mix together the eggs and sugar. Add to the flour mixture. Spread on an ungreased 9x13-inch pan. Bake at 350° for 20 minutes. Spread on jam. Combine remaining ingredients. Mix well. Pour over jam. Bake at 350° for 30 minutes more. When cool, dust with powdered sugar. Cut into squares. Yield 3 to 4 dozen.

Anonymous

Desserts & Sweets

Raisin Honey Cookies

¾ cup honey
¾ cup sugar
¾ cup butter, softened
1 egg
2 cups sifted flour
1 tsp. salt
1 tsp. cinnamon
½ tsp. baking soda
2 cups uncooked rolled oats
1 cup raisins

Combine the honey, sugar, butter and egg. Cream together well. Mix together the remaining ingredients. Add to the creamed mixture. Mix well. Drop by teaspoonfuls onto a greased cookie sheet. Bake at 350° for 10 to 12 minutes, until lightly browned. Yields 6 dozen.

Jane Houston

Apricot and Raspberry Almond Balls

A treat the men especially will love.

½ cup butter
⅓ cup sugar
1 egg, separated
½ tsp. vanilla
1 cup sifted flour
½ tsp. salt
¾ cup chopped almonds
¼ cup apricot preserves
¼ cup raspberry preserves

Cream butter and sugar until light and fluffy. Add egg yolk and vanilla. Mix well. Add flour and salt gradually. Mix well. Roll dough into small balls about 1 inch in diameter. Dip balls in lightly-beaten egg white. Roll in almonds. Place on greased cookie sheets. Press top of each cookie with thumb. Bake at 300° about 24 minutes. Remove from oven. Fill centers with preserves. Dust lightly with powdered sugar. Yields about 2 dozen.

Deborah Holbrook

Desserts & Sweets

Swedish Farm Cookies

A crisp, melt-in-your-mouth treat.

2 cups flour
1 tsp. baking soda
1 cup butter, softened
3/4 cup sugar
1 Tbs. dark corn syrup
1/2 cup chopped nuts

Sift together the flour and baking soda. Cream together the butter and sugar. Add the flour mixture. Beat well. Add the corn syrup to the flour mixture. Stir in the nuts. Form into a roll and wrap in waxed paper. Chill. Slice into 1/4-inch thick pieces and place 1 inch apart on a greased cookie sheet. Bake at 325° to 350° for 10 minutes. Cool for 1 or 2 minutes before removing. Yields about 4 dozen.

Leitzel Malzahn

Saucepan Brownies

1 cup butter or 1/2 cup butter and 1/2 cup margarine
4 squares unsweetened baking chocolate
2 cups sugar
2 tsp. vanilla
3 eggs
1 1/2 cups flour
1/2 tsp. salt
chopped nuts, if desired

Melt butter and chocolate in a saucepan over low heat. Cool. Beat in sugar and vanilla. Add eggs, one at a time. Beat well. Add flour, salt and nuts. Pour into a lightly-greased 9x13-inch baking pan. Bake at 350° for 25 to 35 minutes. Yields 2 dozen.

Ann Hill

Desserts & Sweets

Two Make and Bake Together All-Occasion Desserts

Preparation time for both takes about 45 minutes. Use for bridge parties, showers, graduations or whenever you want an impressive dessert platter.

Lemon Bars

½ cup butter or margarine
1 cup flour
¼ cup powdered sugar
1 cup sugar
2 Tbs. flour
½ tsp. baking powder
2 eggs, beaten
5 to 6 Tbs. lemon juice

Mix together the butter, 1 cup flour and powdered sugar. Pat into the bottom of a well-greased 8x8-inch pan. Bake at 350° for 15 minutes. Combine sugar, 2 tablespoons flour and baking powder. Add eggs and juice. Mix well. Pour over hot, baked crust. Bake 25 minutes longer. Cool. Glaze with additional powdered sugar mixed with a little milk and lemon juice. Cut into 16 squares.

Cheesecake Squares

5 Tbs. butter or margarine
⅓ cup brown sugar
1 cup sifted flour
¼ cup chopped nuts
½ cup sugar
1 8-oz. pkg. cream cheese, softened
1 egg
2 Tbs. milk
1 Tbs. lemon juice
½ tsp. vanilla

Combine butter and brown sugar. Add flour and nuts. Mix well, setting aside 1 cup for topping. Press remainder into bottom of a well-greased 8x8-inch square pan. Bake at 350° for 15 minutes. Blend sugar and cream cheese together until smooth. Add remaining ingredients. Beat well. Pour over hot, baked crust. Sprinkle with reserved topping. Bake 25 minutes longer. Cool and refrigerate. Cut into 16 squares. Yields 32 squares.

JoAnne Schelwat

Desserts & Sweets

Best Butter Cookies

1 cup butter
½ cup sugar
1⅔ cups flour

Cream together the butter and sugar. Add flour. Roll into walnut-sized balls. Flatten with the bottom of a wet glass. An almond, pecan or walnut half may be put on top. Place on cookie sheets. Bake at 350° for 8 to 10 minutes. Yields 3½ dozen.

Ann Hill

Beacon Hill Cookies

1 6-oz. pkg. semi-sweet chocolate chips
2 egg whites
dash of salt
½ cup sugar
½ tsp. vanilla
½ tsp. vinegar
¾ cup chopped walnuts

In a double boiler melt the chocolate chips. Cool. Beat the egg whites and dash of salt until foamy. Gradually add the sugar, beating well after each addition. Beat until stiff peaks form. Beat in the vanilla and vinegar. Fold the egg white mixture into the melted chocolate. Drop by teaspoonfuls on a greased cookie sheet. Decorate with the chopped walnuts, if you wish. Bake at 350° for 10 minutes. Remove immediately. Yields 3 dozen.

Harriet Vick

Desserts & Sweets

Cinnamon Logs

1 cup butter
1 tsp. almond extract
1 Tbs. ground cinnamon
3 Tbs. sugar
2 cups flour
powdered sugar

Put butter, extract, cinnamon and sugar in bowl of a food processor. Using knife blade, process for 20 to 30 seconds. Add flour. Pulse until mixed, 8 to 10 pulses. Remove from bowl. If any flour remains, mix in by hand. Refrigerate. Shape dough into rolls about ½ inch in diameter, 8 to 10 inches long. Cut logs into 1½-inch long pieces. Place on ungreased cookie sheets. Bake at 300° for 20 minutes. Cool slightly before removing from sheets. While still warm, roll in or sprinkle with powdered sugar. Yields 3 dozen.

Lolita Truss

Green Striped Brownies

A rich bar that should be cut and served in small pieces.

1 cup sugar
1 stick margarine
4 eggs
1 cup flour
½ tsp. baking powder
1 16-oz. can chocolate syrup

frosting:
    1 stick margarine, melted
    2 cups powdered sugar
    2 Tbs. milk
    1 tsp. peppermint extract
    green food coloring

glaze:
    1 stick margarine
    1 6-oz. pkg. chocolate chips

Cream sugar and margarine together. Add eggs, one at a time, beating well. Add flour, baking powder and syrup. Pour into a greased jelly roll pan (10½x15½x1-inch). Bake at 350° for 20 minutes. Cool. Mix together the frosting ingredients. Spread over cooled brownies. Refrigerate until set. Melt together the glaze ingredients. Spread over set frosting. Refrigerate. Cut into small bars. Can be frozen either before or after cutting. Yields 40 to 50 bars.

Lynn Falconer

Desserts & Sweets

Diet Gelatin

A lo-cal dessert for calorie watchers.

1 envelope unflavored gelatin
2 cups water
1 pkg. any flavor unsweetened powdered soft drink mix
½ tsp. liquid sweetener

Soften gelatin in ½ cup water. Boil 1½ cups water. Add to gelatin. Add remaining ingredients. Mix well. Pour into ½-cup serving dishes. Serves 4.

Phyllis Weis

Coconut Cream Dessert

½ cup flour
¼ cup butter
¼ cup ground nuts
4 oz. cream cheese, softened
1 8-oz. carton non-dairy whipped topping
½ cup powdered sugar
1 3-oz. pkg. instant coconut cream pudding
1½ cups milk
coconut flakes, toasted

Cut together the flour, butter and nuts as for a pie crust. Press into a 9x9-inch pan. Bake at 350° for 12 to 15 minutes. Cool. Cream together the cheese, sugar and half the whipped topping. Spread over cooled crust. Beat together the pudding mix and milk until thick. Spread over cheese layer. Spread on remaining whipped topping. Sprinkle with coconut. Refrigerate or freeze. Serves 6 to 9.

Sharon Roderick

Desserts & Sweets

Caramel Pumpkin Flan

1   cup light cream
5   eggs
2/3 cup sugar
1 1/4 tsp. pumpkin pie spice or 1 tsp.
    cinnamon, 1/2 tsp. ground ginger,
    1/4 tsp. ground cloves
1/2 tsp. salt
1   16-oz. can pumpkin

caramel crystal sauce:
    1 1/2 cups sugar
    1   cup boiling water
    2   Tbs. butter
    2   Tbs. light corn syrup

Scald cream in a medium-sized saucepan. Combine eggs, sugar, spice and salt. Mix well. Slowly blend egg mixture into cream. Add pumpkin. Mix well. Pour into a well-buttered flan pan or 4-cup mold. Set in a large, shallow pan of boiling water. Bake at 350° for 30 minutes or until center is almost set but soft. Remove at once from water. Cool on a rack. Chill several hours. To make sauce, heat sugar in a heavy frying pan, stirring constantly. Remove from heat. Slowly add water. Blend in butter and corn syrup. Store in refrigerator until ready to serve.

To serve, loosen edges, set in hot water and turn out onto a serving dish. Cover with mounds of whipped cream or encircle with whipped cream. Drizzle top with caramel sauce, which has been warmed just enough to melt the layer of butter that forms on top and has been stirred until well blended.

Serves 6 to 8.

Jean Lindemann

Desserts & Sweets

Creme Brulee

1 qt. *heavy cream*
1 *vanilla bean*
4 Tbs. *white sugar*
pinch of salt
8 *egg yolks*
¾ *to 1 cup light brown sugar*

In a large saucepan, scald cream with vanilla bean. Add sugar. Cook until completely dissolved. In a large bowl, beat egg yolks until a light lemon color. Stir hot cream mixture carefully into yolks adding salt. Stir mixture into a 10-inch shallow baking dish or into 8 ramekins. Place in a pan of hot water. Bake at 350° for 50 to 60 minutes (35 to 40 minutes for ramekins), or until a knife inserted in center comes out clean. Cool. Refrigerate until chilled. Push light brown sugar through a sieve. Spread on top of custard making a ¼-inch thick layer. Broil 4 to 6 inches from element until sugar is caramelized, turning to caramelize evenly. Process takes about 3 to 4 minutes, depending upon degree of caramelization desired. Serve cool. Take spoon and crack crust, serving a piece with custard. You can make custard 2 to 3 days ahead by wrapping well, refrigerating and caramelizing the day of serving. Serves 8.

Carol Lewensohn

Peter's Mousse au Chocolate

A rich dessert that melts in your mouth.

1 6-oz. pkg. *chocolate bits*
2 Tbs. *hot water or strong coffee*
3 *eggs, separated*
2 Tbs. *dark rum or 1 Tbs. coffee and 1 Tbs. Cointreau*
1 Tbs. *sugar*
½ pt. *heavy cream, whipped*

Melt chocolate and water in a double boiler. Add egg yolks. Mix well. Add the rum. Mix well. Beat the egg whites until stiff, adding sugar while beating. Fold into chocolate mixture. Gently fold in the whipped cream. Pour into a decorative serving dish. Chill several hours. Can be topped with additional whipped cream. Serves 6.

Lois Le Vine

Desserts & Sweets

Cranberries Flambe

When serving, darken your dining room to create drama.

1 cup honey
½ cup water
1 tsp. finely shredded orange peel
1 tsp. finely shredded lemon peel
3 cups fresh cranberries
¼ cup brandy
1 qt. vanilla ice cream

Combine honey, water, orange and lemon peels in a large skillet or chafing dish. Add cranberries. Bring to boiling. Boil gently for 5 minutes until skins pop and sauce is slightly thickened. Heat brandy in a small saucepan over low heat until warm. Ignite. Pour over berries. Serve over ice cream. Serves 8 to 10.

Bobbe Blumberg

•

Cranberries were first known as "crane berries" because the cranes living near the bogs used to eat the berries. Cranberries also are known as "bounce berries" because cranberries bounce when they are ripe.

•

A New Look at Blueberries

This can be made a day or two before serving, especially if pie crust isn't on the bottom to get soggy.

4 cups fresh blueberries, washed, de-stemmed, drained
¾ cup water
½ cup sugar
2 Tbs. cornstarch dissolved in ¼ cup water
¼ tsp. cinnamon
1 Tbs. butter
1 Tbs. orange flavored liqueur
¼ cup toasted, slivered almonds
1 cup whipping cream
2 Tbs. sugar
¼ tsp. almond extract
1 9-inch baked pie crust (optional)

Combine sugar and water. Bring to a slow boil. Add 1 cup blueberries. Cook 5 minutes. Puree mixture in a blender in 3 batches. Return to saucepan. Add cornstarch-water mixture and cinnamon. Cook until thickened, about 10 minutes. Blend in butter and Cointreau. Cool. Fold in remaining blueberries and almonds. Put into attractive serving bowl. Refrigerate several hours. Whip cream. Add sugar and almond extract. Put on blueberries just before serving. Or pour into pie crust, if you wish. Serves 6.

Gloria Stanford

Desserts & Sweets

Gateau de Creme aux Fraises
(Cream Cake with Berries)

1   8-oz. pkg. cream cheese,
   softened
¾ cup sugar
3 eggs
¼ tsp. almond extract
1 cup sour cream
½ to 1½ tsp. vanilla
fresh sliced or whole strawberries or 1
   pt. fresh raspberries

Beat together the cream cheese and sugar with an electric mixer. Add eggs one at a time, beating well. Blend in almond extract. Pour into a buttered quiche pan. Bake at 350° for 30 minutes. Cake will puff up a little. Cool 20 minutes. Top with sour cream mixed with vanilla. Bake at 350° for 10 minutes more. Chill. Top with fresh berries or other fruit as available or desired. Serves 6.

Barbara Smilow

Raspberry Ice

A light dessert, colorful for use over the holidays.

1   10-oz. pkg. frozen raspberries in
   syrup
½ cup water
¼ cup sugar
dash of salt
1 tsp. lemon peel
¼ tsp. orange peel
½ cup orange juice
2 to 3 Tbs. ruby port wine
1 Tbs. lemon juice

Combine raspberries, water, sugar and salt in a saucepan. Heat to boiling. Simmer 6 minutes. Press through a small mesh sieve to strain out seeds. Add remaining ingredients to pureed raspberries. Stir well. Freeze until mushy. Beat with mixer. Freeze until firm. Cover to store. Serves 4.

Diane Wright

CATEGORY INDEX

ENTREES: POULTRY

ENTREES: FISH AND SEAFOOD

ENTREES: MEATS

VEGETABLES AND
ACCOMPANIMENTS

ALPHABETICAL INDEX

ORDER FORM

A Taste of Milwaukee may be ordered by mail. Cost is $9.95 per copy plus
$1.50 shipping and handling. Wisconsin residents please add $.50 state sales
tax.

Send to: _____

name

_____

address

_____

city   state   zip

Please make checks payable to: The Muses-Cookbook, and mail to:

> The Muses-Cookbook
> Milwaukee Public Museum
> 800 W. Wells St.
> Milwaukee, WI 53233

. . . .

ORDER FORM

A Taste of Milwaukee may be ordered by mail. Cost is $9.95 per copy plus
$1.50 shipping and handling. Wisconsin residents please add $.50 state sales
tax.

Send to: _____

name

_____

address

_____

city   state   zip

Please make checks payable to: The Muses-Cookbook, and mail to:

> The Muses-Cookbook
> Milwaukee Public Museum
> 800 W. Wells St.
> Milwaukee, WI 53233

ORDER FORM

A *Taste of Milwaukee* may be ordered by mail. Cost is $9.95 per copy plus
$1.50 shipping and handling. Wisconsin residents please add $.50 state sales
tax.

Send to: _____
name

_____
address

_____
city   state   zip

Please make checks payable to: The Muses-Cookbook, and mail to:

The Muses-Cookbook
Milwaukee Public Museum
800 W. Wells St.
Milwaukee, WI 53233

· ·

ORDER FORM

A *Taste of Milwaukee* may be ordered by mail. Cost is $9.95 per copy plus
$1.50 shipping and handling. Wisconsin residents please add $.50 state sales
tax.

Send to: _____
name

_____
address

_____
city   state   zip

Please make checks payable to: The Muses-Cookbook, and mail to:

The Muses-Cookbook
Milwaukee Public Museum
800 W. Wells St.
Milwaukee, WI 53233